Julia Donaldson is one of Britain's most popular children's writers. Three of her rhyming stories, *The Gruffalo*, *Room on the Broom* and *The Snail and the Whale*, have won the Blue Peter Award for the Best Book to Read Aloud. *The Gruffalo* also won the Smarties Prize, and *The Gruffalo's Child* won the Best Children's Book of the Year at the 2005 British Book Awards. After studying Drama at Bristol University, Julia went on to write plays, songs and musicals, and *Play Time* is a collection of her plays for children. Julia now lives in Glasgow but often travels to perform her songs, stories and plays. You can find out more on her website, www.gruffalo.com.

# Julia Donaldson

# PLAY TIME

MACMILLAN CHILDREN'S BOOKS

First published 2006 by Macmillan Children's Books
a division of Macmillan Publishers Limited
20 New Wharf Road, London N1 9RR
Basingstoke and Oxford
www.panmacmillan.com

Associated companies throughout the world

ISBN-13: 978-0-330-44595-5
ISBN-10: 0-330-44595-2

Typeset by Intype Libra Ltd
Printed and bound in Great Britain by
Mackays of Chatham plc, Kent

# Contents

# From Julia

My children, like many others, used to moan when we dragged them out on country walks. But whenever we crossed a bridge over a stream the moaning would cease and be replaced by excited argument: 'It's my turn to be the Troll.' 'No, it's mine.' This was the prelude to the compulsory acting out of their favourite story, *The Three Billy Goats Gruff*.

Most children I know love acting plays as much as they dislike country walks. In my experience, they also love *reading* plays. I discovered this when I was roped into my oldest son's primary school as one of the 'reading helpers'. I would shepherd a little reading group into the empty cookery room where I was supposed to hear them read one at a time while the others 'got on with their work'. It wasn't a great success: the readers were wooden and self-conscious while the others mucked about till it was their turn. I racked my brains for a way of involving and interesting everyone and hit on the idea of plays. Every week I would write a short tailor-made play for a particular reading group. (Unsurprisingly, *The Three Billy Goats Gruff* was one of the first.) I would cast it, initially giving the ablest readers the most demanding roles but then swapping the parts again and again till each child had read each part. Then, with great excitement, we would emerge from the cookery room and present the rest of the class with a dramatic rehearsed reading. As a result, the children's reading improved hugely, and the woodenness was replaced with (sometimes over-the-top) expression.

After this era came to an end, my plays nestled in a drawer until 1993, when the publication of my first book, *A Squash and a Squeeze*, gave me the confidence to send them to an educational publisher. For the next five or so years I was kept busy writing plays for all ages and reading abilities. They were all published separately, and I am excited that many of them are now appearing together for the first time.

The first four plays in the collection, *The Three Billy Goats Gruff*, *The Boy Who Cried Wolf*, *Turtle Tug* and *The Magic Twig*, all based on traditional tales, are for beginner readers and are suitable either for a reading group or for a family. (I remember writing plays as a child for my own family to perform and being furious with my father when he forgot his lines as the woodcutter in *Little Red Riding Hood*.)

*Birthday Surprise*, which was the first play I ever had published, is suitable either for a whole primary-school class or for a group of ten. It's about a spoilt child's birthday party and the machinations of a visiting conjuror, and is very easy to stage with basic props, as are all the plays in the collection.

*The Wonderful Smells* and *Names and Games* are suitable for children of around eight. *The Wonderful Smells* is based on a Chinese traditional story, whereas *Names and Games* is set in a modern school playground and is about bossiness and name-calling.

*Top of the Mops* and *All Gone!* were both written for 'reluctant readers', so have simple vocabulary and sentence structure but cover subjects of interest to children of nine or over. (*Top of the Mops* was inspired by my middle son's teenage rock group.)

*Books and Crooks,* my own favourite, was originally

intended for teenage reluctant readers but I have found that it works very well with a top primary class. It is a comical detective story about the criminal activities of two innocent-seeming old ladies.

The last play in the collection, *Persephone,* is intended for performance by a whole top primary class. It's an exciting kidnap story based on the Greek myth, with three songs in it and a cast of gods, mortals and sea nymphs. I produced it in my youngest son's school, so it has been tried and tested.

Whether you are content to be the smallest Billy Goat Gruff or whether you aspire to be the Ruler of the Underworld, I hope that you will enjoy reading and acting these plays and will share my own love of the bright lights and the greasepaint.

Break a leg!

# The Three Billy Goats Gruff

## A play
## by Julia Donaldson

### Four parts

Suitable for a beginner readers' reading group
or for performance

Running time: Five minutes

# *Characters*

Little Billy Goat Gruff
Middle-sized Billy Goat Gruff
Big Billy Goat Gruff
Troll

# The Three Billy Goats Gruff

## SCENE 1

*[The three Billy Goats Gruff are in a field by a bridge. The Troll is hiding under the bridge.]*

*Little:* Hello! I'm Little Billy Goat Gruff.

*Middle:* I'm Middle-sized Billy Goat Gruff.

*Big:* I'm Big Billy Goat Gruff.

*Troll:* I'm a troll.

*Little:* I like eating grass.

*Middle:* I like eating grass too.

*Big:* So do I.

*Troll:* I like eating goats!

*Little:* Big Billy Goat Gruff?

*Big:* Yes?

*Little:* I don't like this grass.

*Big:*     Why not?

*Little:*   It's all brown.

*Big:*     You're right. It's not very nice.

*Middle:*  But look at that grass over there – that isn't brown.

*Little:*   No, it's green! Let's go and eat it.

*Big:*     Wait!

*Middle:*  Why?

*Big:*     To get to that grass we need to go over the bridge.

*Little:*   So what?

*Big:*     There's a troll under the bridge.

*Middle:*  A troll?

*Big:*     Yes, and he likes eating goats.

*Little:*   Help!

*Middle:*  What can we do?

*Big:*     Just let me think.

*Little:*    I don't like trolls!

*Middle*:    Ssshh! Big Billy Goat Gruff is thinking.

*Little:*    Will he think of something?

*Middle:*    Yes. Now shh!

*Big:*    Come here! This is what we can do!

    *[They whisper together.]*

## SCENE 2

*[Little Billy Goat Gruff starts to cross the bridge. The Troll pops up.]*

*Little:*    *[on the bridge]* Trip-trap, trip-trap, trip-trap.

*Troll:*    Who's that trip-trapping over my bridge?

*Little:*    It's me, Little Billy Goat Gruff.

*Troll:*    You look good. I'm going to eat you!

*Little:*    Oh no, don't eat *me*! Wait for Middle-sized Billy Goat Gruff.

*Troll:*    Why?

*Little:*   He's bigger than me.

*Troll:*   All right then. I'll wait for him

*Little:*   Trip-trap, trip-trap, trip-trap. Green grass, here I come!

*Middle:*   [on the bridge] Clip-clop, clip-clop, clip-clop.

*Troll:*   Who's that clip-clopping over my bridge?

*Middle:*   It's me, Middle-sized Billy Goat Gruff.

*Troll:*   You look good. I'm going to eat you!

*Middle:*   Oh no, don't eat *me*! Wait for Big Billy Goat Gruff.

*Troll:*   Why?

*Middle:*   He's bigger than me.

*Troll:*   All right then, I'll wait for him.

*Middle:*   Clip-clop, clip-clop, clip-clop. Hello, Little Billy Goat Gruff!

*Little:*   Hello! Have some of this green grass.

*Middle:*   Mmmmmmmm, it's so good!

*Big:* [on the bridge] Tramp-stamp, tramp-stamp, tramp-stamp.

*Troll:* Who's that tramp-stamping over my bridge?

*Big:* It's me, Big Billy Goat Gruff.

*Troll:* You look good. I'm going to eat you!

*Big:* That's what you think!

*Troll:* Why, what do *you* think?

*Big:* I think that I'm going to butt you!

[Big Billy Goat Gruff butts the Troll.]

*Troll:* Help! I'm falling into the river. Splosh!

*Big:* Tramp-stamp, tramp-stamp, tramp-stamp.

*Little:* Hello, Big Billy Goat Gruff! Have some of this green grass – it's so good!

*Middle:* Good old Big Billy Goat Gruff. I said he'd think of something and he did!

*Big:* That old Troll won't get us now!

# The Boy
# Who Cried Wolf

### A play
### by Julia Donaldson

### Four parts

Suitable for a beginner readers' reading group
or for performance

Running time: Seven minutes

# *Characters*

Shopkeeper
Tom
Wolf
Baker

# The Boy Who Cried Wolf

*[There are two shops and a hill nearby. One shop is a bakery and the other a grocer's shop. Tom goes into the grocer's shop.]*

Shopkeeper:    Hello, Tom. What do you want?

Tom:    Some milk for my picnic, please. I'm taking my sheep up the hill.

Shopkeeper:    I'd like to be you, up on the hill all day. Here's your milk.

Tom:    Thank you. Oh look!

Shopkeeper:    What?

Tom:    There's a monkey playing with your eggs!

Shopkeeper:    Where? I can't see a monkey.

Tom:    Ha ha! It was just a trick.

Shopkeeper:    You and your tricks! Off you go!

Tom:    I like playing tricks!

Wolf:    *[hiding]* So do I!

*[Tom goes into the bakery.]*

*Baker:*    Hello, Tom. What do you want?

*Tom:*    A cake for my picnic, please.

*Baker:*    I wish I could have a picnic too.

*Wolf:*    Me too – a picnic of sheep!

*Baker:*    Here's your cake.

*Tom:*    Thank you. Oh look!

*Baker:*    What?

*Tom:*    There's a giraffe eating your gingerbread!

*Baker:*    Where? I can't see a giraffe.

*Tom:*    Ha ha! It was just a trick.

*Baker:*    You and your tricks! Off you go!

*Tom:*    That was fun! I do like playing tricks.

*Wolf:*    So do I – and I like eating sheep too!

*Tom:*    Come on, sheep! Up the hill!

*[Tom goes up the hill with the sheep.]*

Tom: Here we are. I'll have my milk, and then I'll play another trick.

*[Tom drinks the milk. Then he runs down the hill, shouting.]*

Tom: Help! Help! There's a wolf eating my sheep!

Shopkeeper: I'm coming, Tom!

Tom: Quick, quick, run!

Shopkeeper: I am running!

Tom: Here we are!

Shopkeeper: I can't see a wolf.

Tom: Ha ha! It was just a trick.

Shopkeeper: That's not funny.

Tom: Don't be cross. You said you wanted to be up on the hill.

Shopkeeper: I'm going to tell your dad about you.

*[The shopkeeper goes away down the hill.]*

*Tom:*    That was fun! I'll have my cake now. Then I'll play another trick.

         *[Tom eats the cake. Then he runs down the hill, shouting.]*

*Tom:*    Help! Help! There's a wolf eating my sheep!

*Baker:*  I'm coming, Tom!

*Tom:*    Quick, quick, run!

*Baker:*  I am running!

*Tom:*    Here we are!

*Baker:*  I can't see a wolf.

*Tom:*    Ha ha! It was just a trick. There isn't one.

Wolf:    *[hiding]* That's what he thinks!

*Baker:*  That's not funny. I'm going to tell your mum.

*Tom:*    No, don't do that. Go back to your shop. There's a crocodile in there, eating up all the cakes.

         *[The baker goes down the hill. The wolf comes out of hiding.]*

*Wolf:*          Good day to you, Tom.

*Tom:*          Oh no, a wolf. Help!

*Wolf:*          And *I'm* going to have a good day too. I do so like sheep for my picnic.

*Tom:*          No, stop! You can't eat my sheep!

                *[Tom runs down the hill, shouting.]*

*Tom:*          Help! Help! There's a wolf eating my sheep!

*Shopkeeper:*   Oh no there isn't. It's just a trick.

*Tom:*          It's not. I'll go and get my dad.

*Shopkeeper:*   He won't come. I've told him about your tricks.

*Tom:*          Oh no! Help! Help!

*Baker:*        What is it?

*Tom:*          There's a wolf eating my sheep!

*Baker:*        Go away, Tom. You can't trick me.

*Tom:*          I'll go and get my mum.

*Baker:* She won't come. I've told her about your tricks.

*Tom:* Oh no! No one will come.

*[Tom runs back up the hill.]*

*Wolf:* Hello, Tom. Thank you for the picnic. I do like sheep. Oh look!

*Tom:* What?

*Wolf:* There's an elephant eating your hat!

*Tom:* Where? I can't see an elephant.

*Wolf:* Ha ha! It was just a trick! Good day to you.

# Turtle Tug

## A play
## by Julia Donaldson

### Four parts

Suitable for a beginner readers' reading group
or for performance

**Running time: Eight minutes**

# *Characters*

Mr Turtle
Elephant
Mrs Turtle
Hippo

# Turtle Tug

*[The setting is a river with two banks and an island in the middle. Elephant lives on one bank and Hippo on the other. The two turtles live on the island.]*

## SCENE 1

*[Elephant is standing on his river bank. Mr Turtle swims across to join him.]*

*Mr Turtle:* Hello, Elephant.

*Elephant:* It's *Sir* Elephant.

*Mr Turtle:* Sorry, *Sir* Elephant. It's Mrs Turtle's birthday tomorrow. Can you come to her party?

*Elephant:* Don't be silly, Turtle.

*Mr Turtle:* I'm not being silly. Mouse can come and Monkey can come. Why can't you?

*Elephant:* Me? A big strong elephant like me, come to a little turtle's party? No thank you.

*Mr Turtle:* All right, Elephant, but you'll miss all the fun.

| | |
|---|---|
| *Elephant:* | It's *Sir* Elephant, and it's no fun for me to mix with weak little animals like you. |
| *Mr Turtle:* | If you say so, *Sir* Elephant. Goodbye! |
| | *[Mr Turtle swims away.]* |

## SCENE 2

*[Hippo is standing on her river bank. Mrs Turtle swims across to join her.]*

| | |
|---|---|
| *Mrs Turtle:* | Hello, Hippo. |
| *Hippo:* | Call me *Madam* Hippo. |
| *Mrs Turtle:* | Sorry, *Madam* Hippo. It's my birthday tomorrow. Can you come to my party? |
| *Hippo:* | Don't be silly. |
| *Mrs Turtle:* | I'm not being silly. Goat can come and Rabbit can come. Why can't you? |
| *Hippo:* | Me? A bit strong hippo like me, come to a little turtle's party? No thank you. |
| *Mrs Turtle:* | All right, Hippo, but you'll miss all the fun. |

*Hippo:*    It's *Madam* Hippo, and it's no fun for me to mix with weak little animals like you.

*Mrs Turtle:*    If you say so, *Madam* Hippo. Goodbye!

   *[Mrs Turtle swims away.]*

## SCENE 3

*[Mr and Mrs Turtle are at home on Turtle Island.]*

*Mrs Turtle:*    How did you get on?

*Mr Turtle:*    Mouse can come and Monkey can come, but not Elephant.

*Mrs Turtle:*    Why not?

*Mr Turtle:*    He says he's too big and strong.

*Mrs Turtle:*    He's so snooty!

*Mr Turtle:*    How did *you* get on?

*Mrs Turtle:*    Goat can come and Rabbit can come, but not Hippo.

*Mr Turtle:*    Why not?

*Mrs Turtle:*    She says she's too big and strong.

| | |
|---|---|
| *Mr Turtle:* | Just like Elephant. How can we stop the two of them being so snooty? |
| *Mrs Turtle:* | Let me think. Do we have a long rope? |
| *Mr Turtle:* | Yes. |
| *Mrs Turtle:* | And a sharp stone? |
| *Mr Turtle:* | I can find one. |
| *Mrs Turtle:* | Good. Then I think there is a way! |

## SCENE 4

[*Mr Turtle has a rope. He swims across the river to join Elephant.*]

| | |
|---|---|
| *Mr Turtle:* | Hello, Elephant. |
| *Elephant:* | It's *Sir* Elephant! What is it now? |
| *Mr Turtle:* | I'd like to have a tug-of-war with you. |
| *Elephant:* | Me? A big strong elephant like me, have a tug-of-war with a weak little turtle? |
| *Mr Turtle:* | I'm just as strong as you! |
| *Elephant:* | Ha ha! All right, we'll try it. |

22

| | |
|---|---|
| *Mr Turtle:* | Good. Take this end of the rope and when I shout 'Go!' you pull. |

*[Mr Turtle swims back across the river and meets Mrs Turtle on Turtle Island. He gives her the other end of the rope.]*

| | |
|---|---|
| *Mr Turtle:* | Here's the end of the rope. |
| *Mrs Turtle:* | Thank you. |

*[Mrs Turtle swims to Hippo's bank of the river.]*

| | |
|---|---|
| *Mrs Turtle:* | Hello, Hippo! |
| *Hippo:* | It's *Madam* Hippo. What do you want now? |
| *Mrs Turtle:* | I'd like to have a tug-of-war with you. |
| *Hippo:* | Me? A big strong hippo like me have a tug-of-war with a weak little turtle? |
| *Mrs Turtle:* | I may be little but I'm not weak. |
| *Hippo:* | Ha ha! All right, we'll try it. |
| *Mrs Turtle:* | Take this end of the rope and when I shout 'Go!' you pull. |

*[Mrs Turtle swims back to Mr Turtle on Turtle Island.]*

*Mr Turtle:*    All right?

*Mrs Turtle:*    Yes.

*Mr Turtle:*    Let's shout then.

*Mr and Mrs Turtle:*    GO!

*[Elephant and Hippo both pull the rope.]*

*Elephant:*    Mr Turtle isn't all that weak.

*Hippo:*    I didn't think Mrs Turtle was so strong!

*Elephant:*    I'll have to pull harder.

*Hippo:*    If I don't pull harder she'll pull me into the river!

*Mrs Turtle:*    Have you got the sharp stone?

*Mr Turtle:*    Here it is.

*Mrs Turtle:*    Good. Let's cut the rope.

*[They cut the rope, and Elephant and Hippo*

*both fall over backwards. Mr Turtle swims to Elephant's bank.]*

**Mr Turtle:** Hello, Sir Elephant. Are you all right?

**Elephant:** Yes thank you, but I got a surprise. You *are* strong, just as strong as me!

**Mr Turtle:** I said so, didn't I?

**Elephant:** Yes, you did. I'm sorry I was so snooty.

**Mr Turtle:** That's all right, Sir Elephant.

**Elephant:** You can just call me Elephant.

**Mr Turtle:** All right then, Elephant. See you at the party!

*[Mrs Turtle swims to Hippo's bank.]*

**Mrs Turtle:** Can I help you up, Madam Hippo?

**Hippo:** Thank you – and you don't have to call me *Madam*. I didn't think you were so strong. I'm sorry I was so snooty.

**Mrs Turtle:** That's all right, Hippo. So are you going to come to my party?

*Hippo:*       Yes please. And what do you want for your birthday?

*Mrs Turtle:*   How about a new rope!

# The Magic Twig

## A play
## by Julia Donaldson

## Four parts

Suitable for a beginner readers' reading group
or for performance

**Running time: Seven minutes**

# Characters

The Wind
Anna, a farmer
An innkeeper
A cook

# The Magic Twig

## SCENE 1: The Wind's House

*[The Wind is running about, blowing. There is a knock at the door.]*

*Wind:* Come in!

*Anna:* *[coming in]* Hello, Wind . . .

*Wind:* Blow! Blow! Down you go! *[He blows Anna down.]*

*Anna:* Help! Stop it!

*Wind:* I'm sorry. I do so like a good blow! Now, what is it?

*Anna:* It's about my apple trees. All the apples have fallen off. Did you blow them down?

*Wind:* Me? Apples? Oh yes, I did blow down one or two apples.

*Anna:* Not just one or two – all of them! They were just little apples. Now I can't sell them.

*Wind:* Oh dear, I'm sorry. Here, have this.

29

| | |
|---|---|
| *Anna:* | A twig? What good is that? |
| *Wind:* | You'll see. Take it and say:<br>'Little twig, little twig,<br>Give me apples, red and big.' |
| *Anna:* | 'Little twig, little twig,<br>Give me apples, red and big.' |
| *Wind:* | Now look in your pockets. |
| *Anna:* | Two big red apples! That's magic! Thank you, Wind. |
| *Wind:* | Go home now, and you'll have apples for ever and ever. |

## SCENE 2: An Inn

*[The innkeeper and cook hear a tap at the door. It is Anna who is on her way home from the Wind's house.]*

| | |
|---|---|
| *Innkeeper:* | Come in! |
| *Anna:* | *[coming in]* Can I stay here tonight? |
| *Cook:* | Yes, you can. But what have you got there? |
| *Anna:* | It's a twig. The Wind gave it to me. |

Cook:        What for?

Anna:        You'll see. Take it and say:
             'Little twig, little twig,
             Give me apples, red and big.'

Cook:        'Little twig, little twig,
             Give me apples, red and big.'

Anna:        Now look in your pockets.

Cook:        Apples!

Innkeeper:   Big red apples!

Cook:        That's magic!

Anna:        I'm going to have apples for ever and ever.

Innkeeper:   That's good. But you look sleepy now.

Cook:        Yes, why don't you go to bed? That's your bed-
             room.

Anna:        Thank you, I will. [She goes into the bedroom.]

Innkeeper:   Are you thinking what I'm thinking?

Cook:        Yes. Let's steal the twig.

*Innkeeper:*    We can swap it for this one.

*Cook:*        Now we'll have apples for ever and ever!

## SCENE 3: The Wind's House

*[The Wind is running about, blowing.]*

*Wind:*       Blow! Blow! Down you go!
             Oh for a good blow!

             *[There is a knock at the door.]*

*Wind:*       Come in!

*Anna:*       *[coming in]* Now look here, Wind . . .

*Wind:*       Blow! Blow! Down you go!

*Anna:*       Stop that!

*Wind:*       Don't be cross. I did give you the magic twig!

*Anna:*       Yes, but when I got home it didn't work.

*Wind:*       Oh dear. Here, have this.

*Anna:*       A jug of water – what good is that?

*Wind:*       It's magic water. One drop of it can turn into a

32

river. Now you'll have lots of fish for ever and ever.

*Anna:*       Is this a trick?

*Wind:*       No, it's not.

*Anna:*       Thank you, Wind. *[She takes the jug and is going out.]*

*Wind:*       The water can do one other thing.

*Anna:*       What's that?

*Wind:*       It can drown anyone who has played a trick on you.

## SCENE 4: The Inn

*[There is a knock at the door.]*

*Innkeeper:*   Come in.

              *[Anna comes in.]*

*Cook:*       Oh, it's you.

*Anna:*       Hello! What a lot of apples you've got!

*Cook:*       Yes. But what have you got there?

*Anna:*      A jug of water. The Wind gave it to me.

*Cook:*      What for?

*Anna:*      It's magic water. One drop can turn into a river. I'm going to have lots of fish for ever and ever.

*Innkeeper:*      Let's try it in my garden!

*Cook:*      Yes, let's!

*Anna:*      The water can do one other thing.

*Innkeeper:*      What's that?

*Anna:*      It can drown anyone who has played a trick on me.

*Cook:*      Oh help!

*Anna:*      But no one here has played a trick on me, so that's all right. Let's try it now.

*Innkeeper:*      No, please don't!

*Anna:*      Why not?

*Innkeeper:*      Here, you can have your twig back.

*Anna:*      My twig! What, you took it?

*Cook:*      Yes, but we're sorry!

*Innkeeper:*  Please don't drown us!

*Anna:*      All right. But no more tricks!

*Cook:*      Thank you, thank you!

*Innkeeper:*  Do you want a bed for the night?

*Cook:*      Or some food?

*Anna:*      No, not in your house! I'm going home to eat lots of fish and apples!

# All Gone!

## A play
## by Julia Donaldson

### Four parts

Suitable for reluctant readers aged 8–11

Running time: Seven minutes

# Characters

A waitress
Four customers
An old lady

# All Gone!

*[The scene is a self-service cafe. There is a counter, four tables, an entrance door and a door marked 'Toilet'. Four customers are queuing up at the counter.]*

Waitress:      Yes, what do you want?

Customer 1:    Some soup, please.

Waitress:      Here you are. That's eighty pence, please.

Customer 2:    Can I have some chips?

Waitress:      Here you are. That's eighty pence. Next, please.

Customer 3:    I'd like a cake, please.

Waitress:      Here you are. That's eighty pence. This job is so boring. Next, please.

Customer 4:    A cup of tea, please.

Waitress:      Here you are. That's—

Customer 4:    Eighty pence?

Waitress:      How did you guess?

*[An old lady comes into the cafe. No one sees her.]*

**Customer 1:** *[now sitting at a table with the bowl of soup]* Oh dear, I need a spoon for my soup. *[He gets up and leaves the table.]*

**Old lady:** This soup looks good. *[She picks up the bowl and starts to drink it.]*

**Customer 1:** *[at the counter]* Can I have a spoon for my soup, please?

**Waitress:** Here you are.

**Customer 1:** Thank you.

**Old lady:** That soup *was* good. But I'm still hungry! *[She gets up and leaves the table.]*

**Customer 1:** *[back at his table]* Hey! Where is my soup?

**Customer 2:** *[sitting at a table with his chips]* I need some salt for my chips. *[He gets up and leaves the table.]*

**Old lady:** These chips look good! *[She starts to eat them.]*

**Customer 2:** *[at the counter]* Can I have some salt, please?

Waitress: Here you are.

Customer 2: Thank you.

Old lady: Those chips *were* good. But I'm still hungry. *[She leaves the table.]*

Customer 2: *[back at his table]* Hey! Where are my chips?

Customer 3: *[sitting at a table with her cake]* I need a fork for my cake. *[She gets up and leaves the table.]*

Old lady: This cake looks good! *[She starts to eat it.]*

Customer 3: *[at the counter]* Can I have a fork, please?

Waitress: Here you are.

Customer 3: Thank you.

Old lady: That cake *was* good. But now I'm thirsty. *[She leaves the table.]*

Customer 3: *[back at her table]* Hey! Where is my cake?

Customer 4: *[at a table, taking a sip of tea]* Oh dear, I forgot to put any milk in my tea. *[He gets up and leaves the table.]*

*Old lady:* Oh good! I like black tea. *[She starts to drink it.]*

*Customer 1:* *[back at the counter]* Where is my soup?

*Waitress:* Don't ask me.

*Customer 2:* Where are my chips?

*Waitress:* I don't know!

*Customer 3:* Where is my cake?

*Waitress:* Don't ask me. *I don't know!*

*Customer 4:* Can I have some milk, please?

*Waitress:* *DON'T ASK ME! I DON'T KNOW!*

*Customer 4:* What do you mean, you don't know? You must know if you've got some milk.

*Waitress:* Sorry. Here you are.

*Old lady:* That tea was good. But now I need to go to the toilet. *[She leaves the table and goes into the toilet.]*

*Customer 4:* *[back at his table]* Hey! Where is my tea?

# All Gone!

Customer 1: *[still at the counter]* Who's been eating my soup?

Customer 2: Who's been eating my chips?

Customer 3: Who's been eating my cake?

Waitress: Oh shut up! This isn't *Goldilocks and the Three Bears.*

Customer 4: *[joining the other customers]* Who's been drinking my tea?

Waitress: That's it! I hate this job. I'm leaving! *[She goes towards the door.]*

*[The customers run after her. The old lady comes out of the toilet, still unseen.]*

Customer 1: *[calling after the waitress]* Hey! Stop!

Customer 2: Come back!

Customer 3: I want my money back!

Customer 4: So do I! *[They run out of the shop after the waitress.]*

Old lady: What are they making such a fuss about? *I* think it's a very good cafe.

# Birthday Surprise

## A play
## by Julia Donaldson

### Ten parts
(can be expanded to include a whole class)

Suitable for middle primary

Running time: About twenty minutes

# Characters

Stuart, the birthday boy. *He is cross, grumpy and rude. Nothing is ever right for him and one of his favourite words is 'boring'.*

Stuart's mum. *She has a hard job trying to keep everyone happy and stop Stuart being rude to his friends.*

Rachel
Joe
Ajax
David
Samantha
Jaswinder
Ellen
} *These are some of the friends Stuart has invited to his party. They are all more polite than he is, and better at enjoying themselves. They each have four or five things to say.*

The other children at the party. *They don't have lines to say by themselves, but they join in the games and spells. There can be as many or as few of them as you like.*

Mr E. *He is not just an ordinary conjuror – he's a real magician. He likes children, but not when they're rude about his tricks.*

# Birthday Surprise

*[Stuart is in his sitting room with Mum and some of his friends, including Ajax, Samantha, Ellen and Joe. There is a table with a floor-length cloth on it. Under this a toy rabbit must be hidden.]*

| | |
|---|---|
| *Mum:* | Well, nearly everyone's here. Shall we start the party games? |
| *Stuart:* | I don't want to play games. I want to have tea. |
| *Mum:* | We can't have tea till everyone's here. Shall we play The Farmer's in his Den? |
| *Children:* | Yes! |
| *Stuart:* | No, that's stupid. |
| *Mum:* | You can be the farmer, Stuart, as it's your birthday. |
| *Stuart:* | I don't want to be the farmer. I want to be the dog. |
| *Mum:* | All right, then – you be the farmer, Ajax. Off you go. |
| *Children:* | *[in a circle]* The farmer's in his den. |

The farmer's in his den.
Ee, I, Ee, I, the farmer's in his den.

*[The doorbell rings.]*

Mum:      There's the doorbell. I'll go. You carry on playing.

*[Mum goes out.]*

Children:      The farmer wants a wife.
The farmer wants a wife.
Ee, I, Ee, I, the farmer wants a wife.

*[Mum comes in with Rachel.]*

Mum:      It's Rachel, Stuart.

Rachel:      Happy birthday, Stuart.

Stuart:      Where's my present?

Mum:      Stuart, don't be so greedy!

Rachel:      Here you are, Stuart.

Stuart:      *[unwrapping the present]* It's not very big. It's a book. That's boring!

Mum:      Stuart, don't be so rude! Thank you very much,

Rachel. Would you like to play The Farmer's in his Den?

*Rachel:*  Yes, please.

*[Rachel joins the circle.]*

*Joe:*  Who are you going to choose for your wife, Ajax?

*Ajax:*  Samantha.

*[The doorbell rings again.]*

*Mum:*  There's the bell again. I'll go. You carry on playing.

*[Mum goes out.]*

*Children:*  The wife wants a child.
The wife wants a child.
Ee, I, Ee, I, the wife wants a child.

*[Mum comes in with David.]*

*Mum:*  It's David, Stuart.

*Stuart:*  Where's my present?

*Mum:*  Stuart, really!

David:        Here you are, Stuart.

Stuart:       *[unwrapping the present]* I know what this is. A boring old football. I've got one already.

Mum:          Stuart, don't be so rude! Thank you very much, David. Would you like to play The Farmer's in his Den?

Stuart:       Yes, please.

              *[David joins the circle.]*

Ajax:         Who are you going to choose for your child, Samantha?

Samantha:     Ellen.

              *[The doorbell rings again.]*

Mum:          That must be Jaswinder. She's the last one. I'll go. You carry on playing.

              *[Mum goes out.]*

Stuart:       It's not fair. I want to be the child. It's my birthday.

Samantha:     You said you wanted to be the dog.

| | |
|---|---|
| *Stuart:* | I'm sick of this boring game anyway. I want to have tea. |
| | *[Mum comes in with Jaswinder.]* |
| *Mum:* | It's Jaswinder, Stuart. Now, do be polite. |
| *Jaswinder:* | Happy birthday, Stuart. |
| *Stuart:* | Where's my present? |
| *Mum:* | STUART! BEHAVE YOURSELF! |
| *Jaswinder:* | Here you are, Stuart. |
| *Stuart:* | *[opening the present]* It feels like a car. Yes, it is. Is it radio-controlled? |
| *Jaswinder:* | No. |
| *Stuart:* | It's boring, then. |
| *Mum:* | If you go on like this you'll go up to your room and have no birthday cake. Thank you very much, Jaswinder. Everyone's here, then. |
| | *[The doorbell rings again.]* |
| *Mum:* | Who can that be? I'll go and see. |

*[Mum goes out.]*

*Ellen:*      What are we having for tea, Stuart?

*Stuart:*      Mum wouldn't let me see. I bet there are cucumber sandwiches. I hate them.

*Ajax:*      What sort of cake have you got?

*Stuart:*      I don't know. I bet it's a boring old round one.

*[Mum comes in.]*

*Mum:*      Children, I've got a very special surprise for you. Everyone be quiet.

*Stuart:*      I don't want a surprise, I want tea.

*Mum:*      Not yet, Stuart. Now, when you're all quiet the conjuror will come in.

*Stuart:*      I don't want a conjuror, I want—

*Children:*      BE QUIET!

*[Mum opens the door and Mr E comes in.]*

*Mr E:*      Good afternoon, my friends. My name is Mister E.

Stuart:     That's a stupid name.

Rachel:     What does the E stand for?

Mr E:       Aha, it's a mystery.

Mum:        Mystery, Mister E – that's funny, isn't it? Now, children, you sit and watch Mr E's show while I get the tea on the table.

            *[Mum goes out. The children sit on the floor.]*

Mr E:       Now, my friends, my magic wand is telling me that one of you has a birthday today.

Stuart:     I bet it was my mum who told you, not your wand at all.

Mr E:       It's you, isn't it? You're the one.

Stuart:     So what?

Mr E:       So I am inviting you to help me perform Trick One!

Stuart:     I don't want to.

Mr E:       Very well, I shall choose again. What is your name, young friend?

Rachel:     Rachel.

Mr E:       Would you like to help me perform Trick One, Rachel?

Rachel:     Yes, please.

Mr E:       Then step forward and hold this hat while I wave my wand. Would our other friends like to help me say the magic spell?

Children:   Yes!

Stuart:     No.

Mr E:       [tapping the magic hat] Very well, repeat after me:
            Abracadabra and rat-tat-tat,
            What's inside the magic hat?

Children:   Abracadabra and rat-tat-tat,
            What's inside the magic hat?

Mr E:       I'm ready to grab it.
            I think it's a . . .

            [He puts his hand into the hat and pulls out a rabbit.]

Children:   RABBIT! [They clap.]

| | |
|---|---|
| *Stuart:* | That's stupid. Anyone could do that. I bet you couldn't make a *monster* come out of the hat. |
| *Mr E:* | We shall see, but first I shall need a new helper. What is your name, young friend? |
| *Joe:* | Joe. |
| *Mr E:* | Would you like to help me perform Trick Two, Joe? |
| *Joe:* | Yes, please. |
| *Mr E:* | Then step forward and take the hat from Rachel, if you please. Are you ready for the next spell, my friends? |
| *Children:* | Yes! |
| *Stuart:* | I bet it will be the same as the last one. |
| *Mr E:* | Abracadabra and vampire bat,<br>What's inside the magic hat? |
| *Children:* | Abracadabra and vampire bat,<br>What's inside the magic hat? |
| *Mr E:* | It's coming to get us. |

*[Some of the children back away.]*

*Mr E:*    I think it's a . . .

*[He puts in his hand and pulls out a lettuce.]*

*Children:*    LETTUCE! *[They laugh.]*

*Stuart:*    That's stupid. You said it would be a monster.

*Mr E:*    Aha, I was tricking you! I told you it was a trick, didn't I?

*David:*    The rabbit will like the lettuce, anyway.

*Stuart:*    I bet it was in the hat all the time.

*Mr E:*    Let us move on to Trick Three and a new helper. What is your name, young friend?

*Ellen:*    Ellen.

*Mr E:*    Would you like to help me perform Trick Three, Ellen?

*Ellen:*    Yes, please.

*Stuart:*    It's not fair; I want to be the helper. It's my birthday.

*Mr E:*    Very well, as Trick Three is such a tricky trick, I shall have two helpers instead of one. Step forward, Stuart and Ellen. I need one of you to go under that table.

Stuart: I will! It's my birthday. *[He goes under the table.]*

Mr E: Are you ready for the next spell, my young friends?

Children: Yes!

Mr E: Abracadabra and Auntie Mabel, What is under the magic table?

Children: Abracadabra and Auntie Mabel, What is under the magic table?

Mr E: Now, Ellen, I need you to look under the table.

*[Ellen goes behind the table and lifts the cloth.]*

Mr E: Get ready to grab it. I think it's a . . .

*[Rachel pulls a rabbit out from under the table.]*

Children: RABBIT! *[They clap.]*

Joe: Where's Stuart?

*Ellen:*    He's not there any more.

*David:*    He must have turned into the rabbit!

            *[Enter Mum.]*

*Mum:*      Are you enjoying the show, children?

*Children:* Yes!

*Mum:*      The birthday tea's ready. *[She looks around.]* Where's Stuart?

*Ellen:*    *[holding the rabbit]* Here he is.

*Mum:*      Don't be silly – that's a rabbit.

*Ajax:*     Yes – Stuart's turned into a rabbit.

*Mum:*      Do stop joking. Where is he?

*Mr E:*     He is here in front of your eyes, madam. So very nice and quiet.

*Mum:*      Oh no! This is terrible! I want my little boy back.

*Mr E:*     Do not fear, madam. He will change back in an hour or so.

*Mum:*        Are you sure?

*Mr E:*       As sure as my name is Mr E.

*Mum:*        And are you sure he'll be exactly the same as before?

*Mr E:*       More or less, madam, more or less.

*Mum:*        *[alarmed]* What do you mean, more or less?

*Mr E:*       I just mean he might be a little bit . . . different.

*Mum:*        Different? In what way?

*Mr E:*       Well, usually with Trick Three the children end up just a little bit . . . nicer.

*Children:*   Hooray!

*Samantha:*   But do we have to wait an hour for our tea?

*Mum:*        No, let's have it now. It should be nice and peaceful. *[To Mr E]* Would you like to have some tea too?

*Mr E:*       Yes, please, madam. And perhaps our rabbit friends would like to come too.

*Jaswinder:*  Do rabbits like birthday cake?

*Mr E:* No, my friend, but there is one thing which they love.

*David:* What's that?

*Mr E:* Cucumber sandwiches!

*[They all go out of the room to have tea.]*

# Names and Games

## A play
## by Julia Donaldson

### Four parts

Suitable for middle primary

Running time: About twenty minutes

# Characters

Robin. *He is a very bossy boy. He has plenty of good ideas for exciting games but always wants to take the best parts himself. He is also quite fat and sometimes gets teased because of this.*

Jamie. *He is Robin's best friend but is beginning to be fed up with Robin's bossy ways.*

Helen. *She is very keen for Tanim to be her best friend and gets quite jealous if Tanim plays with anyone else or lets other people into their games. She is not bossy like Robin is, but she sometimes tries to hurt people by calling them names.*

Tanim. *She has no trouble making friends. She likes playing with Helen but she would rather play with a bigger group of people. She is not very good at sticking up for herself or other people.*

*The four children are all in the same year at school.*

# Names and Games

*[Each scene of the play takes place in the school playground during a different playtime on the same day.]*

## SCENE 1: Morning Play

*[Enter Robin and Jamie.]*

| | |
|---|---|
| *Robin:* | Hi, Jamie. |
| *Jamie:* | Hi, Robin. What shall we play today? |
| *Robin:* | Robin Hood, of course. |
| *Jamie:* | All right. I'll be Robin Hood then. |
| *Robin:* | No you can't. I'm Robin Hood. I'm always Robin Hood, remember? |
| *Jamie:* | That's not fair. Why should you always be Robin Hood? |
| *Robin:* | Because my name really is Robin. |
| *Jamie:* | Well, who shall I be then? |
| *Robin:* | Little John, of course. |

| | |
|---|---|
| *Jamie:* | But I'm sick of being Little John all the time. He just gets bossed about by Robin Hood. |
| *Robin:* | All right, you can be Friar Tuck then. |
| *Jamie:* | Who's he? |
| *Robin:* | He's this big fat guy who eats all the time. |
| *Jamie:* | That sounds more like you. |
| *Robin:* | I'm not fat. |
| *Jamie:* | I didn't say you were fat, I just said— |
| *Robin:* | *[noticing Helen and Tanim coming towards them]* Be quiet, Little John – someone's coming! Let's hide, then we can spring out on them and take all their gold. |
| | *[Robin and Jamie hide. Enter Helen and Tanim.]* |
| *Tanim:* | Hi, Helen. |
| *Helen:* | Hi, Tanim. What shall we play today? |
| *Tanim:* | How about Tunnel Tig? |

| | |
|---|---|
| *Helen:* | I've forgotten how you play that. |
| *Tanim:* | You know, it's that game where you crawl under people's legs to set them free when they've been caught. |
| *Helen:* | Oh yes, that's good. Who's going to be It? |
| *Tanim:* | Let's dip. *[She 'dips', starting with Helen.]*<br>Ibble obble,<br>Black bobble,<br>Ibble obble out!<br>I'm it! |
| *Helen:* | Hey, wait a minute – we can't play that! |
| *Tanim:* | Why not? |
| *Helen:* | Well, if you catch me, who's going to crawl under my legs to set me free? |
| *Tanim:* | We could try and get some more people. |
| *Helen:* | No, I like playing with just you. Let's think of a different game. |
| | *[Jamie and Robin spring out.]* |
| *Jamie:* | Give us all your gold or we'll tie you up! |

| | |
|---|---|
| *Robin:* | No, I say that – I'm Robin Hood, remember? |
| *Jamie:* | Go on then. |
| *Robin:* | Give us all your gold or we'll tie you up! |
| *Helen:* | Go away, you two. We haven't got any gold. |
| *Tanim:* | We're not playing Robin Hood anyway. |
| *Jamie:* | What are you playing then? |
| *Tanim:* | We were going to play Tunnel Tig but we haven't got enough people. Do you two want to play? |
| *Helen:* | No, we're not having them. Robin's too bossy. |
| *Robin:* | I don't want to play stupid old Tunnel Tig anyway. Hey, look, Jamie – I mean, Little John – there are some deer over there in the forest! Let's get them! |
| | *[Robin and Jamie run off.]* |
| *Helen:* | I know! Let's play bank robbers! |

| | |
|---|---|
| *Tanim:* | How do you play that? |
| *Helen:* | Well, one person is the bank robber and one person is the banker, and one person is the policewoman . . . |
| *Tanim:* | But we've only got two people. We can't play that. |
| *Helen:* | Oh dear. |
| *Tanim:* | We'll have to get some more people. |

*[Jamie and Robin spring out again.]*

| | |
|---|---|
| *Jamie:* | Run for your lives, you two deer! We're going to shoot you with our bows and arrows! |
| *Robin:* | No, I have to say that – I'm Robin Hood, remember? |
| *Jamie:* | Go on then. |
| *Robin:* | Run for your lives, you two deer! We're going to shoot you with our bows and arrows! |
| *Helen:* | Go away, you two. We're not deer. |

Robin:       Yes you are – I just heard you say, 'Oh dear' to Tanim.

Helen:       Oh, very funny. Anyway, we've already told you, we're not playing Robin Hood.

Jamie:       Why won't you?

Tanim:       Yes, let's, Helen. We haven't got enough people for any of our games.

Helen:       No, I'm not playing with Robin. I told you, he's too bossy.

Tanim:       I like running games.

Helen:       All right, race you to the shed, then.

*[Helen and Tanim race off.]*

Jamie:       I managed to shoot those deer, Robin.

Robin:       No you didn't, *I* did. I'm Robin Hood, remember? I'm the best one at shooting arrows. You can cook the deer for our supper if you like.

Jamie:       Why don't you cook them?

Robin:       I can't cook them, I'm the boss.

| | |
|---|---|
| *Jamie:* | Well, I've had enough of you bossing me about. |

*[The bell rings.]*

| | |
|---|---|
| *Jamie:* | There's the bell. And if you think I'm playing Robin Hood again next playtime, you're wrong! |

## SCENE 2: Lunchtime Play

*[Enter Helen and Tanim.]*

| | |
|---|---|
| *Tanim:* | What can we play with only two people? |
| *Helen:* | Let's play the yes and no game. |
| *Tanim:* | How do you play that? |
| *Helen:* | Well, one person asks questions and the other one has to answer them without saying yes or no. |
| *Tanim:* | All right. I'll ask the questions then. Er . . . is your name Helen? |
| *Helen:* | It is. |
| *Tanim:* | And . . . do you like fish and chips? |

| | |
|---|---|
| *Helen:* | I do. |
| *Tanim:* | Are you my best friend? |
| *Helen:* | Of course I am. |
| *Tanim:* | You're too good at this game! Let's think . . . Do you like Jamie? |
| *Helen:* | He's all right sometimes. |
| *Tanim:* | Do you like Robin? |
| *Helen:* | He's much too bossy. Oh no! Here he comes! |

*[Enter Robin and Jamie.]*

| | |
|---|---|
| *Tanim:* | You just said no! You're out! |
| *Jamie:* | Hi, Helen. Hi, Tanim. |
| *Tanim:* | Are you two still playing Robin Hood? |
| *Jamie:* | No, and I'm not ever playing it again. I'm sick of always being Little John. |
| *Robin:* | I know, let's play Robinson Crusoe instead. We could all play that. |

| | |
|---|---|
| *Helen:* | No, Tanim's playing with just me. |
| *Tanim:* | Hold on, Helen. Let's find out how you play it – it could be good. |
| *Robin:* | Well, Robinson Crusoe gets shipwrecked and he ends up on this desert island. He has a friend called Man Friday. You can be him, Jamie. |
| *Jamie:* | Why can't I be Robinson Crusoe? |
| *Robin:* | Is your name Robin or something? |
| *Jamie:* | What does Man Friday do? |
| *Robin:* | Well, he sort of follows Robinson Crusoe around and does what he says. |
| *Jamie:* | This sounds just like Robin Hood. |
| *Robin:* | It's not a bit like Robin Hood, silly. We're on an *island*. Look, there are sharks all around us! Helen and Tanim can be the sharks. |
| *Helen:* | No, we're not playing your stupid game. |

| | |
|---|---|
| *Tanim:* | Oh, let's, Helen. It sounds better than the yes and no game. |
| *Helen:* | All right then. |
| *Jamie:* | Watch out, sharks, I'm going to harpoon you! |
| *Robin:* | No, I'm Robinson Crusoe, I have to say that. Watch out sharks, I'm going to harpoon you, and Man Friday will cook you for supper! |
| *Helen:* | Oh no you won't. We'll eat you for *our* supper! |
| *Robin:* | No, no, you can't do that! |
| *Tanim:* | Why not? |
| *Robin:* | That's not in the story. |
| *Helen:* | Well, we're changing the story, aren't we, Tanim? |
| *Tanim:* | Yes, we're going to get you! |
| | *[Tanim and Helen start to chase after the boys.]* |

| | |
|---|---|
| *Robin:* | No, I'm not playing if you're going to change the story. Come on, Jamie. |
| *Jamie:* | No, why should I? I'm fed up with you, Robin. It's always, 'Come on, Jamie. Do this, Jamie. Do that, Jamie.' I'm staying here with the girls. |
| | *[The bell rings.]* |
| *Robin:* | All right, but I won't play with you next playtime. |
| *Jamie:* | I don't care. I'd rather play with Helen and Tanim. You're much too bossy, Robin! |

## SCENE 3: Afternoon Play

*[Enter Robin and Jamie.]*

| | |
|---|---|
| *Robin:* | Hi, Jamie. What shall we play? |
| *Jamie:* | Nothing! I'm playing with Helen and Tanim, remember? |
| *Robin:* | All right, but don't expect me to play with you ever again. *[He turns away.]* |
| *Jamie:* | Where are you going? |

| | |
|---|---|
| *Robin:* | Oh, I'll probably go and play football with the big boys. |

*[He wanders off. Enter Helen and Tanim.]*

| | |
|---|---|
| *Tanim:* | Hi, Jamie. We're going to play 'What's the Time, Mr Wolf?'. |
| *Jamie:* | Can I be Mr Wolf first? |
| *Helen:* | Let's see. *[She 'dips', starting with Jamie.]* <br> Dip, dip. <br> Sky blue. <br> Who's It? <br> Not you! <br> You're Mr Wolf, Tanim. Come on, Jamie. |

*[They walk along behind Tanim.]*

| | |
|---|---|
| *Jamie and Helen:* | What's the time, Mr Wolf? |
| *Tanim:* | Four o'clock. |
| *Jamie and Helen:* | What's the time, Mr Wolf? |
| *Tanim:* | Half past eleven. |
| *Jamie and Helen:* | What's the time, Mr Wolf? |

| | |
|---|---|
| *Tanim:* | Dinner time! *[She chases them and catches Helen.]* Got you, Helen! Your turn to be Mr Wolf. Come on, Jamie. |
| *Jamie and Tanim:* | What's the time, Mr Wolf? |
| *Helen:* | Eight o'clock. |
| *Jamie and Tanim:* | What's the time, Mr Wolf? |
| *Helen:* | Quarter past five. |
| *Jamie and Tanim:* | What's the time, Mr Wolf? |
| *Helen:* | Dinner time! *[She chases them and catches Tanim.]* Got you, Tanim! |
| | *[Enter Robin, looking rather miserable.]* |
| *Robin:* | Can I play? |
| *Helen:* | No! You're too bossy. |
| *Robin:* | Oh, go on. |
| *Jamie:* | I thought you were going to play football with the big boys. |
| *Robin:* | *[rather embarrassed]* They wouldn't let |

me. They said I was too young, and they said I was . . . oh, never mind.

Tanim:       What did they say you were?

Robin:       They said I was a rotten runner.

Helen:       Well, you are! Robin is a slowcoach, Robin is a slowcoach!

Jamie:       Don't be mean. He's not a slowcoach.

Helen:       Well, he can't play anyway, can he, Tanim?

Tanim:       Why don't we give him another chance?

Helen:       No, we don't want a fat old slowcoach playing with us. Round Robin, Round Robin!

Jamie:       *[getting cross]* Don't be so nasty. He's my friend.

Tanim:       Oh go on, let him.

Helen:       No, he can't. Silly Robin Redbreast! Silly Robin Redbreast!

Jamie:       *[really angry now]* I think you're being

really horrible. I'm not going to play with you any more.

Helen: Don't, then!

Tanim: *[pleading]* Oh yes, do!

Helen: It's nearly the end of playtime anyway. Come on, Tanim, let's see if we can be the first in the line.

*[Helen and Tanim go off.]*

Robin: Thanks, Jamie. You were really nice.

Jamie: Well, I was getting fed up with 'What's the time, Mr Wolf?' anyway. It's a bit of a baby game, and I never even got to be Mr Wolf.

Robin: Will you play with me now, then?

Jamie: It all depends.

Robin: Depends on what?

Jamie: On whether you're going to boss me about all the time.

Robin:                 I won't, I promise. I know, you can choose which game to play.

Jamie:                 All right then.

*[There is a pause while Jamie thinks.]*

Robin:                 Remember, if there's anyone called Robin in it I have to be him, because my name really is Robin.

Jamie:                 *[looking pleased]* That's just given me a brilliant idea.

*[The bell rings.]*

Jamie:                 Oh, there's the bell.

Robin:                 Never mind, we can play it tomorrow. What is it?

Jamie:                 Batman and Robin!

*[He runs off, followed more slowly by Robin who is looking thoughtful.]*

# The Wonderful Smells

A play
by Julia Donaldson

Seven parts
(but can be expanded)

Suitable for middle–top primary

Running time: Twenty-five minutes

# Characters

Li Hua, *an eight-year-old girl from a poor family. Although she can't read, she is bright and has a good imagination.*

Li Chang, *her brother, aged six. He often squabbles with Li Hua, but is always ready to spring to her defence.*

Shen Ying, *a mean woman. She serves the food in the Full Moon Cafe. She is very polite to anyone rich, but is rude to the children because they are poor.*

Dong Da, *a kind, rich man. He is friendly and generous to the Li family.*

Mrs Li, *the children's mother. She has a hard job feeding her family, especially now her husband has hurt his foot and can't work.*

Pang Bo, *a mean man. He cooks the food in the cafe and is always cheating the customers.*

Tian Guan, *a judge.*

Cafe customers and other people in the court *can be included if you want to add more actors.*

# The Wonderful Smells

## SCENE 1

*[Outside the Full Moon Cafe. Li Hua enters, carrying firewood. Li Chang, her brother, follows, but stops outside the cafe and sniffs the air.]*

**Li Hua:**    Hurry up, Li Chang! This firewood's so heavy. Don't you want to get home?

**Li Chang:**    I'm coming.

**Li Hua:**    No you're not; you're just standing there, sniffing the air.

**Li Chang:**    Can you smell what I can?

**Li Hua:**    Mmm! Roast duck!

**Li Chang:**    And bamboo shoots!

**Li Hua:**    There's something else too . . . something sweet.

**Li Chang:**    Mangoes! What wonderful smells! Where are they coming from?

**Li Hua:**    The Full Moon Cafe, of course.

*Li Chang:*    Shall we play at being rich people?

*Li Hua:*    All right. Let's pretend we can read the menu.

*[They go right up to the cafe and look at the menu.]*

*Li Chang:*    I'm going to start with fried shrimps.

*Li Hua:*    You're a silly little shrimp yourself. Why have shrimps when there's turtle soup on the menu?

*Li Chang:*    I'll have that too.

*Li Hua:*    I'm going to have steamed goose.

*Li Chang:*    *You're* a goose! Roast duck is much nicer.

*Li Hua:*    Let's have both. And can you smell the moon cakes? We'll have some of those too.

*Li Chang:*    We'll eat and eat till we're as fat as Dong Da.

*[Shen Ying comes out of the cafe, looking angry.]*

*Shen Ying:*    Well? Are you coming in or not?

*Li Chang:*    We can't.

*Li Hua:*     We've got no money.

*Shen Ying:*     What do you think you're doing, then?

*Li Chang:*     Just looking at the menu.

*Li Hua:*     And smelling the wonderful smells!

*Shen Ying:*     What a cheek! You think you can just stand here smelling our expensive food when you've got no money?

*Li Hua:*     Why not? Smelling is free, isn't it?

*Shen Ying:*     That's what *you* think, is it? Off you go, before I bring you out a bill. *[She goes back into the cafe.]*

*Li Chang:*     Did you smell those wild mushrooms?

*Li Hua:*     Yes . . . and those dumplings! Mmmm!

*[Enter Dong Da.]*

*Li Chang:*     Here *comes* a dumpling!

*Li Hua:*     Shh! It's Dong Da.

*Li Chang:*     He really *is* rich.

*Dong Da:* Good evening, children. How is your father?

*Li Chang:* Not very well.

*Li Hua:* He cut his foot with an axe, and now he can't work till it gets better.

*Dong Da:* I'm sorry to hear that. Give my best wishes to your mother.

*[Shen Ying comes out of the cafe with a bucket of scraps. She sees the children.]*

*Shen Ying:* What? Still here? Be off with you or I'll empty this rubbish over you.

*Dong Da:* Come, come, Shen Ying, they're not doing any harm.

*Shen Ying:* Oh, sir, I didn't see you. Good evening, sir, and a thousand more good evenings. May the gods give you long life and good health. May your purse always be full. May you—

*Dong Da:* All right, all right, Shen Ying, that's enough. Is my table ready?

*Shen Ying:* Yes, sir.

84

*Dong Da:* Good evening, children, and I hope your father is better soon.

*[Shen Ying holds open the door as Dong Da goes into the restaurant. She empties the rubbish into the street and glares at the children, then goes inside.]*

*Li Hua:* Come on, Li Chang, we really must go. Just one more sniff!

*Li Chang:* A big one, to last us till we get home.

*[They take a big sniff and go off.]*

## SCENE 2

*[Inside the Lis' house the children and Mrs Li are finishing their evening meal.]*

*Li Chang:* Is there any more corn porridge?

*Mrs Li:* No, it's all gone.

*Li Chang:* I'm still hungry.

*Li Hua:* So am I.

*Mrs Li:* There are still some pickled turnips.

*Li Chang:*    They're so dull.

*Li Hua:*    Let's pretend they're something different. Mine's a sweet pancake.

*Li Chang:*    Mine's a moon cake.

*Li Hua:*    *[pointing out of the window]* Look, there's the real moon! It's a full one.

*Li Chang:*    No it isn't.

*Li Hua:*    It is.

*Li Chang:*    It isn't.

*Li Hua:*    It *is* full, isn't it, Mother?

*Mrs Li:*    Not quite. It will be full in two days. That's when the autumn moon festival is.

*Li Chang:*    Oh good, the moon festival! We'll be having moon cakes!

*Mrs Li:*    Not this year, I'm afraid.

*Li Chang:*    But we *always* have moon cakes when it's the festival.

Mrs Li:     I'm sorry, but till your father's foot gets better there's no money.

Li Hua:     I thought you were doing some washing for those rich people.

Mrs Li:     Yes, but they don't pay much. That reminds me, there's a basket of clothes to take back to them. Who's going to take it?

Li Hua:     Li Chang can.

Li Chang:   No, I went last time.

Li Hua:     You didn't.

Li Chang:   I did.

Li Hua:     You didn't.

Li Chang:   Let's toss a coin.

Li Hua:     There isn't a coin to toss, silly.

Mrs Li:     Stop arguing, you're giving me a headache. You go, Li Hua.

Li Hua:     [sulkily] All right, but Li Chang will have to go next time.

*[She takes the basket of clothes and goes out].*

## SCENE 3

*[Outside the Full Moon Cafe. Li Hua is carrying the basket of clothes. She stops to sniff the air. Dong Da comes out.]*

Dong Da:    Hello, it's my little friend again! I hope you haven't been here all this time?

Li Hua:    No, I've been having my supper.

Dong Da:    What did you have?

Li Hua:    Corn porridge and pickled turnips.

Dong Da:    That doesn't sound very exciting. I tell you what, take this coin and go in and buy some moon cakes for your family.

Li Hua:    Oh, thank you, sir! But you've given me too much money.

Dong Da:    Take the change home to your mother. I'm sure she could do with it.

Li Hua:    *Thank* you!

           *[She goes into the restaurant, and Dong Da goes on his way.]*

## SCENE 4

*[Inside the Full Moon Cafe. Pang Bo is at the counter. Li Hua enters.]*

Pang Bo:     Yes, what do you want?

Li Hua:      I want some moon cakes, please. Five of them.

Pang Bo:     They cost one chien each, you know. I hope you've got some money.

Li Hua:      Yes I have, I've got a whole liang. That's the same as ten chien.

Pang Bo:     Let's see.

Li Hua:      Here it is.

Pang Bo:     Huh! I suppose you've been picking pockets.

Li Hua:      No, I haven't.

Pang Bo:     Well, as long as it ends up in *my* pocket it's all the same to me. What kind of moon cakes do you want?

Li Hua:      What kinds do you have?

*Pang Bo:*    Fruit, nut or bean curd.

*Li Hua:*     I'll have fruit ones . . . no, nut. I don't know, they *all* look so good.

*Pang Bo:*    Hurry up and make up your mind.

*Li Hua:*     They *smell* good too! I know, I'll have two fruit, two nut and one bean curd.

*Pang Bo:*    That's right, make things difficult for me. Let's have your money, then.

*Li Hua:*     Here you are.

*Pang Bo:*    Now, take the cakes and be off with you. *[He gives them to her.]*

*Li Hua:*     Thank you. But what about my change?

*Pang Bo:*    Oh, that! Here you are, then, five chien.

              *[Enter Shen Ying.]*

*Shen Ying:*  Wait a minute! That's one of the children I was telling you about.

*Pang Bo:*    What, the ones that were hanging around outside?

*Shen Ying:*    Yes, smelling all our smells for free.

*Pang Bo:*    But you said they had no money.

*Shen Ying:*    That's what *she* told me. You little liar!

*Li Hua:*    I'm *not* a liar! I didn't have any money then, but Dong Da gave me some.

*Shen Ying:*    The fat old fool!

*Pang Bo:*    Never mind if he's a fool, as long as we get his money!

*Li Hua:*    It's *my* money now.

*Pang Bo:*    Not for long, it won't be. You owe it to us, for all those smells you've been swallowing.

*Shen Ying:*    Yes. Hand over those coins.

*Li Hua:*    I won't! Smelling is free. *[She runs out.]*

*Shen Ying:*    *[calling after her]* We'll see about that.

*Pang Bo:*    Yes, and we'll see what the judge has to say about it.

## SCENE 5

*[The next day, inside the Lis' house.]*

Li Hua:     Stop nibbling your moon cake, Li Chang. You won't have any left for the festival tomorrow.

Li Chang:   Well, I'll eat yours then!

Li Hua:     Oh no you won't!

Li Chang:   In any case, Mother will buy us some more with all that money you gave her. Where is she?

Li Hua:     She's in with Father. She's seeing if he can read that letter that came for me today.

            *[Enter Mrs Li from behind a ragged curtain. She holds a letter and looks worried.]*

Li Hua:     Well, could he read it?

Mrs Li:     Most of it.

Li Chang:   Who is it from?

Mrs Li:     It's from the judge.

Li Chang:   The judge! What does he say?

| | |
|---|---|
| *Mrs Li:* | He says that Li Hua is to go to court today. And she's to bring five chien with her. |
| *Li Chang:* | Five chien! But that's all the money she brought back yesterday. Are they going to take it away from her? |
| *Mrs Li:* | We'll have to see. |
| *Li Chang:* | That's *stealing*! If those Full Moon people get the money I'll get it back! |
| *Li Hua:* | How will you do that? |
| *Li Chang:* | I'll get a spear and shield and I'll fight them! |
| *Mrs Li:* | Calm down, Li Chang. Wait and see what the judge says. |
| *Li Chang:* | I'll ride a dragon into the cafe and breathe fire over them! |
| *Mrs Li:* | That's *enough*, Li Chang. If you carry on like that in court you'll end up behind bars. |

## SCENE 6

*[The Courtroom. The judge (Tian Guan), Li Hua, Li Chang, Mrs Li and her younger child, Shen Ying, Pang Bo and Dong Da are all in the room.]*

*Judge:*       And now, the last case of the day. Is Li Hua in court?

*Li Hua:*       *[standing up]* Yes, sir, I'm here.

*Judge:*       Good. Now, Li Hua, you have been accused of robbery. How old are you?

*Li Hua:*       I'm eight, sir.

*Judge:*       Eight. That is very young to begin a life of crime.

*Li Chang:*    She's not a robber! How dare he say that!

*Mrs Li:*      *[whispering]* Shh! He *hasn't* said so. Be quiet and listen.

*Judge:*       Are Pang Bo and Shen Ying in court?

*Pang Bo:*     *[standing up]* Yes, sir.

*Shen Ying:*  *[standing up]* Yes, sir.

*Judge:*       Good. Now, I understand you are the owners of the Full Moon Cafe.

*Pang Bo:*     That's right, sir.

*Judge:*       And you are accusing Li Hua of stealing from your cafe?

*Shen Ying:*   Yes, sir.

*Li Chang:*   *They're* the robbers!

*Judge:*   Silence in court! Now, Pang Bo, what are you saying that the girl stole?

*Pang Bo:*   She took some money, sir, and didn't give it back.

*Judge:*   How much money?

*Pang Bo:*   Five chien.

*Judge:*   So you are telling me that Li Hua took five chien and didn't give it back. What do you say to that, Li Hua?

*Li Hua:*   It was *my* money, sir. I bought some moon cakes and the money was my change. Pang Bo gave it to me!

*Judge:*   The five chien was your change, you say. Is this true, Pang Bo?

*Pang Bo:*   Well, in a way.

*Shen Ying:*   But it was a mistake! He shouldn't have given it to her.

*Judge:*    Explain yourselves.

*Shen Ying:*    Well, it's like this, sir. Our cafe is one of the best in town.

*Pang Bo:*    Yes, and our food is very expensive. A dish of steamed goose costs three liang.

*Shen Ying:*    No, three and a *half* liang.

*Pang Bo:*    Does it?

*Shen Ying:*    Don't you remember, we put all the prices up the other day?

*Pang Bo:*    Oh, yes, of course. But may I say, sir, that if *you* would like to come and eat we could make a special price for you.

*Judge:*    Please stick to the point.

*Shen Ying:*    I was just getting to it. The thing is, this girl has been standing around outside the cafe, smelling all the expensive food.

*Pang Bo:*    Yes, and she hasn't paid us anything. Not a single chien!

*Shen Ying:*    She's been stealing our smells!

*Judge:*      What do you say to that, Li Hua? Is it true that you have been smelling the food from the Full Moon Cafe?

*Li Hua:*      Yes, sir, but I can't help it. I pass by there every day. And anyway, smelling is free, isn't it?

*Judge:*      You must let *me* be the judge of that.

*Shen Ying:*      What a good judge!

*Li Chang:*      I don't like this judge.

*Judge:*      Li Hua, I have another question for you. Did you like the smell of the food?

*Li Hua:*      Yes, sir.

*Judge:*      And do you still have the five chien?

*Li Hua:*      Yes, sir, but . . .

*Judge:*      There are no buts about it.

*Pang Bo:*      Good! He's going to make her pay!

*Shen Ying:*      *[whispering]* That was a brilliant idea of yours to offer him a special price for a meal! Don't let him off *too* much, will you?

*Pang Bo:*     *[whispering]* Don't worry, I'll charge him double for his wine!

*Judge:*     I have here a bag.

*Shen Ying:*     It's a money bag!

*Judge:*     Li Hua, I want you to put the five chien into the bag.

*Li Hua:*     But, sir . . .

*Judge:*     I thought I said no buts. Take the bag, Li Hua.

*Pang Bo:*     *What* a good judge!

*Li Chang:*     He's a terrible judge!

*Judge:*     Now, put the money into the bag.

*Li Hua:*     Do I have to?

*Judge:*     Yes.

*Li Chang:*     No! Stop! This isn't fair! You're as bad as them! I'm going to run you down with a chariot!

*Mrs Li:*     Be quiet, Li Chang. He could put you in prison.

*Li Chang:*     I'll put *him* in prison!

*Judge:* Silence in court! Now, is all the money in the bag?

*Li Hua:* Yes.

*Judge:* Good. I want you to give the bag to me, Li Hua.

*[Li Hua gives him the bag.]*

*Judge:* Thank you. Now I am going to shake this bag of coins. *[He shakes it.]* Did you hear the coins jingling in the bag, Pang Bo?

*Pang Bo:* Yes, sir.

*Judge:* Did you hear them, Shen Ying?

*Shen Ying:* Yes, sir. Thank you, sir.

*Judge:* And did you both like the jingling sound?

*Pang Bo:* Oh yes, sir.

*Shen Ying:* It's one of our favourite sounds, isn't it, Pang Bo?

*Pang Bo:* It certainly is.

*Judge:* I'm glad to hear that. So, Li Hua liked the smell of your food, and you liked the sound of her coins jingling. Come here, Li Hua. You can have your money back now. *[He gives her the bag.]*

*Pang Bo:* But it's *our* money!

*Shen Ying:* It's our pay for the smells!

*Judge:* No. Your pay for the smells was the *sound* of the money.

*Pang Bo:* But . . .

*Judge:* No buts about it! Let the girl go free. The court is finished for today, and tomorrow is a holiday.

*[The judge goes out.]*

*Shen Ying:* What a terrible judge.

*Pang Bo:* He can forget about that special offer!

*[They go out.]*

*Li Chang:* What a good judge! I'm going to be a judge like that when I'm grown up.

*[Dong Da comes over to the family.]*

*Dong Da:* I must say that was better than being at the theatre. Congratulations, my little friend.

100

*Li Hua:*     Thank you.

*Dong Da:*    And how is your husband, Mrs Li?

*Mrs Li:*     His foot is quite a lot better today. He's begin-
              ning to walk about on it.

*Dong Da:*    Good. It's the Moon Festival tomorrow. May I
              take your family out for a meal?

*Mrs Li:*     Thank you, you're very kind.

*Li Chang:*   Can I have fried shrimps and roast duck and
              moon cakes?

*Dong Da:*    You can have whatever you like. But I must
              warn you of one thing.

*Li Hua:*     What's that?

*Dong Da:*    We *won't* be going to the Full Moon Cafe!

# Top of the Mops

## A play
## by Julia Donaldson

### Four parts

Suitable for top primary
or for reluctant readers aged 10–14

Running time: Twenty minutes

# Characters

Andy Miller, *a teenage rock musician*
Carol Miller, *Andy's mother, an estate agent*
Doreen Blanket, *a cleaner*
Spike, *a teenage singer*

# Top of the Mops

[The play is set in the hallway of the Millers' home. There is a window, a front door, and three more doors, leading to the kitchen, the studio and the broom cupboard.]

## SCENE 1: Wednesday, early evening

[Andy is sitting by the phone, with a paper on his lap. He dials a number.]

Andy:    Hello, I'd like to put an advert in your paper. 'Singer needed to join new band. Phone 483 5593.' That's it. OK. Thank you. Goodbye.

Carol:    [coming out of the kitchen, sounding cross] Andy, the freezer's been unplugged.

Andy:    What? Oh, sorry, Mum, I needed to plug my new guitar in somewhere.

Carol:    What's wrong with your studio? Do you want me to turn it back into a spare room?

Andy:    No, of course not. The studio was just a bit . . . crowded, that's all.

Carol:    In other words it was a complete tip, as usual.

*Andy:*  I'm sorry, Mum. I meant to plug the freezer back in.

*Carol:*  Well, it's too late now. You'll just have to have soggy beef burgers and melted ice cream for supper.

*Andy:*  I've *said* I'm sorry.

*Carol:*  And *what's* this banana skin doing on the floor?

*Andy:*  I don't know – the can-can, maybe.

*Carol:*  Ha ha, very funny.

*Andy:*  Keep your hair on, can't you?

*Carol:*  How *can* I, when I get back from work to find the house looking like this?

*Andy:*  Well, it's not all me. What about your bedroom?

*Carol:*  My bedroom is like Buckingham Palace compared with your studio. Now go and tidy it!

*Andy:*  I'll do it later.

*Carol:*  You'll do it now. Why are you always so lazy?

Andy:      [going out of the front door] I must take after
           you.

           [Carol throws the banana skin at him as he goes
           out.]

Carol:     He's right really. I hate housework. [She picks
           up the paper.] What's this? Evening News.
           Hmmmm. [She dials a number.] Hello, could I
           put an advert in, please? 'Cleaner wanted
           urgently. Phone 483 5593.' Thank you.
           Goodbye.

## SCENE 2: Saturday Morning

[The phone rings. Andy comes out of the studio to answer it.]

Andy:      Hi, Andy Miller here.

Doreen:    [on the phone] Hello, dear, my name's Doreen
           Blanket. I'm ringing about the job.

Andy:      Oh great! Um . . . have you done this sort of
           thing before?

Doreen:    Oh yes, dear, I've worked for ever so many dif-
           ferent people.

Andy:      That's good. Who have you been with, then?

*Doreen:* Let's see . . . The Browns, the Robinsons . . .

*Andy:* I haven't heard of them.

*Doreen:* The Stones . . .

*Andy:* The Stones! Really? That's amazing! Er . . . What sort of stuff do you like doing?

*Doreen:* I'll do whatever needs doing – as long as it's not too heavy, that is.

*Andy:* Oh no, we're not into heavy metal or anything.

*Doreen:* That's good, because I've got a bad back. I can't do a lot of lifting. The last place I worked, they wanted me to lift these heavy metal dustbins.

*Andy:* *[puzzled]* Really? How strange.

*Doreen:* Yes, they were a bit. By the way, there's something I ought to warn you about.

*Andy:* What's that?

*Doreen:* I do like to sing.

*Andy:* Well, I should hope so!

Doreen: You don't mind, then? That's good, because the last people didn't like it at all.

Andy: [*suddenly a bit worried*] Oh dear. Well, I'd need to hear you of course. Could you come round today? At about two? It's 4 Vernon Gardens, by the way.

Doreen: I'll be there!

Andy: That's great! See you at two then, Doreen. Goodbye!

Carol: [*coming out of the kitchen*] Andy, you haven't cleared away the breakfast things.

Andy: OK, OK, I'll do it.

[*He goes into the kitchen. The phone rings. Carol answers it.*]

Carol: Hello, Carol Miller speaking.

Spike: [*on the phone*] Oh, hi, my name's Spike. I'm phoning about the job.

Carol: How wonderful! Have you done this sort of work before, Spike?

Spike: Do you mean with a mike or without?

Carol:    With *Mike*, did you say? No, I don't think we need Mike as well. We're not that big, you know.

Spike:    Who have you got, then?

Carol:    Just the one boy, Andy – mind you, that's quite enough!

Spike:    Is he the drummer or what?

Carol:    How *did* you guess? Yes, he is. I'm afraid he's not very tidy – the studio is a terrible mess.

Spike:    I don't mind that.

Carol:    Oh, you sound *wonderful*, Mike.

Spike:    It's Spike.

Carol:    Spike, of course – Mike's the other one, isn't he?

Spike:    By the way, I do quite a bit of writing.

Carol:    Good for you, Spike! I can tell you're a bright lad. Just don't carve your name on the furniture, will you? *[She laughs.]*

Spike:    *[sounding a bit confused]* No. Er . . . where do you live?

*Carol:*     We're at 4 Vernon Gardens. You couldn't come round today, Spike, could you? At about two?

*Spike:*     Sure, I'll be there.

*Carol:*     That's terrific. Goodbye!

## SCENE 3: 1.45 p.m.

*[The doorbell rings and Carol answers it.]*

*Carol:*     Hello! You must be Spike.

*Spike:*     That's right. I'm sorry, I'm a bit early.

*Carol:*     Not at all – I'm just *so* glad to see you!

*Spike:*     By the way, I forgot to ask what you call yourselves.

*Carol:*     I thought I told you – Miller.

*Spike:*     Just Miller? Do you think that's catchy enough?

*Carol:*     Well, I'm not going to start changing my name – not even for you, Spike!

*Spike:*     No, OK. Er . . . where's the studio then?

Carol:     The studio? Are you sure you want to start there?
           It's in a terrible state, I'm afraid.

Spike:     I don't mind.

Carol:     Oh, you *wonderful* young man! It's that door
           there. And all the stuff you'll need is in this cup-
           board. I'll just pop out to the shops if that's all
           right?

Spike:     What, *now*?

Carol:     I won't be long.

Spike:     OK, then.

           *[Carol goes out. Spike opens the broom cup-
           board.]*

Spike:     I can't see any mikes or anything in here. Maybe
           they're behind all this cleaning stuff. *[He takes
           out the Hoover, brooms, mop, etc.]* Oh well, I'll
           have a look in the studio.

           *[Spike goes into the studio. Andy comes in
           through the front door.]*

Andy:      Amazing! Mum's got the Hoover out for once.

           *[The doorbell rings and Andy answers it.]*

Andy:      Oh hi, are you Doreen?

Doreen:    That's me, dear. I see you're all ready for me! Oh, that's a very nice Hoover you've got there. It's the latest model, isn't it?

Andy:      I don't know.

Doreen:    Where shall I plug it in?

Andy:      Hey, you don't need to do that. I thought you were going to sing!

Doreen:    Oh, you are a one! I do like a bit of music while I work, I must admit.

Andy:      Do you know any blues numbers?

Doreen:    No, dear, nothing like that. It's the shows I like. *The Sound of Music*, that's got some lovely songs in it, hasn't it?

Andy:      Well, it's not really my scene.

Doreen:    Then there's *Oliver*, of course. 'Where is Love?' – that's my favourite.

Andy:      Do you like *Cats*?

Doreen: Not really, dear; they shed their hair all over the furniture, you see.

Andy: *[sounding doubtful]* Yes, well, why don't we go into the studio anyway? Maybe we could try out some Stones songs.

*[From the studio comes the faint sound of a guitar being strummed.]*

Doreen: It sounds like there's someone in there already.

Andy: Probably my mum. She's always nosing around.

Spike: *[singing softly in the studio]*
Woke up this morning.
Never felt so bad . . .

Doreen: She's got a very low voice, hasn't she?

Andy: That's not Mum. *[He looks through the keyhole, then whispers.]* It's a bloke! It must be a burglar!

Doreen: *[Whispering]* You don't say! Shall we go in and tackle him?

Andy: No, he could be dangerous. Look, I'll watch the door while you phone the police.

Doreen: Here – have a broom. *[She hands him a broom,*

*then dials 999.]* Police, please. Hello, we've got a burglar.

*[Carol returns with the shopping. She sees Andy with the broom.]*

Carol:      *[in a loud voice]* Andy, what are you doing?

Andy:       Shhhhh!

Doreen:     *[on the phone]* What was that? Where am I calling from? Four Vernon Gardens.

Carol:      And what's this woman doing using our phone?

Andy:       Mum, there's a burglar in the studio!

*[The door of the studio opens and out comes Spike, carrying two drumsticks. Andy grabs hold of him.]*

Andy:       Not so fast! Those are *my* drumsticks!

Carol:      Don't be silly – that's not a burglar, it's the new cleaner.

Doreen:     *[dropping the phone in surprise]* No it's not, it's my Spike!

Spike:      *[to Doreen]* Mum! What are you doing here?

| | |
|---|---|
| *Carol:* | Really, Spike, fancy asking your mum round to use the phone the second my back's turned. |
| *Spike:* | I didn't ask her – I don't know what she's doing here. |
| *Carol:* | A likely story! And look – you've just left all the cleaning things lying in a heap! |
| *Doreen:* | What's going on, Spike? How do you know these people anyway? And what do you think you're doing messing their house up like this? |
| *Carol:* | He's *supposed* to be cleaning it, not messing it up. |
| *Doreen:* | *[to Andy]* So you'd already found someone to do the cleaning! Well, I like that! You could have told me. |
| *Spike:* | I'm not supposed to be cleaning. I'm supposed to be singing! |
| *Doreen:* | Well, that makes more sense, I must say. He's got a lovely voice, my Spike. It runs in the family. |
| *Andy:* | *[letting go of Spike]* Do you like blues? |
| *Spike:* | Sure. |

Carol: What's going on? I don't understand.

Doreen: I think I'm beginning to. Let's go back a bit – who put the advert in the paper?

Carol: I did.

Andy: No, I did.

Doreen: So there were *two* ads – one for a cleaner and one for a singer. My son Spike here wanted the singing job but you thought he was the cleaner. Am I making sense, dear?

Carol: Yes, go on!

Doreen: Well, then I came round to do the cleaning, only your Andy tried to get me singing in his studio.

Andy: Only Spike was there already. We thought he was a burglar.

Doreen: And we phoned the police – what a hoot!

Carol: I think I get it. There's just one thing that's puzzling me, though.

Doreen: What's that, dear?

Carol: Your face – I feel sure I've seen you before somewhere.

Doreen: I seem to recognize you too. It's going back a bit,
though.

Carol: Wasn't it just before I had Andy?

Doreen: And I was expecting Spike.

Carol: That's it!

Doreen: The hospital baby classes!

Carol: Do you remember that plastic doll we had to
bath?

Doreen: Weren't you the one who kept on dropping her?

Carol: Yes! And you were the one who was always
singing!

Doreen: And do you remember the party after the babies
were born?

Carol: Yes, of course! Andy was so *red* – well, purple,
really, like a little wrinkled plum. So sweet!

Andy: Mum, shut up!

Doreen:     And poor old Spike had that dreadful nappy rash.

Spike:      Stop it, Mum!

Carol:      And then Andy was sick all over that woman with the twins.

Andy:       *Mum!*

Spike:      It's no good. We'll never stop them now.

Andy:       Do you want to come into the studio and try out a couple of songs?

Spike:      Good idea.

            *[Andy and Spike go into the studio.]*

Carol:      You were wonderful – you mopped up all the sick!

Doreen:     Mrs Mop, that's me! Now, dear, I'm just itching to get my hands on your beautiful Hoover.

Carol:      You're *still* wonderful!

Doreen:     You don't mind if I sing, do you?

*Carol:* Not at all. You couldn't clean the cooker as well, could you? It's filthy, I'm afraid.

*Andy:* *[coming out of the studio with Spike]* Hey, Mum, there's a police car outside the house.

*[They all go to the hall window and look out.]*

*Carol:* So there is – and two policemen are getting out of it.

*Doreen:* And a sniffer dog as well – isn't he lovely?

*Carol:* I wonder where they're going?

*Andy:* Look, they're coming up the front steps.

*Everyone:* Oh no!

*[There is a loud ring at the bell.]*

# Books and Crooks

A play
by Julia Donaldson

Five parts

Suitable for top primary
or for reluctant secondary readers

Running time: Thirty minutes

# Characters

Oliver Tremble, *forty, the librarian of Boring-by-Sea library, set in his ways and fond of tea.*

Robin Banks, *twenty-two, a trainee librarian, very keen.*

Homer Lott, *sixty-five, who spends most of his time in the library where he enjoys reading all the bad news in the papers.*

Crystal Ball, *seventy-three* } *Two ladylike but rather*
Charity Ball, *seventy-one* } *mysterious sisters.*

# Books and Crooks

*[All the scenes are set in Boring-by-Sea library.]*

## SCENE 1: Friday, 1 December

*[Robin knocks at the door. Oliver comes out of the kitchen and goes to the door. He has a cup of tea in his hand.]*

Oliver:    We don't open till ten.

Robin:    But I'm Robin Banks!

Oliver:    There aren't any banks here to rob. This is a library.

Robin:    No, no, no! My *name* is Robin Banks. I'm the new trainee librarian. I'm here for two weeks.

Oliver:    Oh, it's you! Sorry, I forgot you were coming. I'll let you in. *[He puts down his tea and unlocks the door.]* I'm Oliver Tremble.

Robin:    Are you really? I'm all of a tremble too, but that's because it's my first day.

Oliver:    No, no! Not 'all of a tremble', Oliver Tremble. That's my name.

123

*Robin:* Oh, of course – you're the head librarian, aren't you?

*Oliver:* I'm the *only* librarian. Would you like a cup of tea?

*Robin:* No thanks. I'd like a look round.

*Oliver:* Well, there's not much to look at really. There are the books. Here's the computer. The kettle's next door. What else do you need to know?

*Robin:* Let's think. Er . . . do you have many events?

*Oliver:* Events? Well, now and then someone comes and changes a book. Is that what you mean?

*Robin:* No, I mean events like . . . well, story-telling, talks, book clubs . . . er . . . puppet shows.

*Oliver:* Oh no, nothing like that. This is Boring-by-Sea, you know, not London or New York. It's not a very eventful library.

*Robin:* Still, it's nice and cosy.

*Oliver:* Yes, it's so cosy you have to pinch yourself to stay awake.

*Robin:* Can I do anything?

Oliver: You can put these newspapers on that table if you like.

Robin: Jolly good! *[He puts the papers on the table.]*

Oliver: Are you sure you don't want any tea?

Robin: No thanks. I say, it's ten o'clock. Shall I unlock the door?

Oliver: You are keen, aren't you? All right then, here's the key.

Robin: Thank you, Mr Tremble.

*[Robin opens the door. Enter Homer.]*

Robin: Good morning.

Homer: It looks like rain to me.

Robin: I'm Robin Banks, the new trainee.

Homer: I'm Homer Lott.

Robin: You're home a lot, are you? Then it must make a nice change coming here.

Oliver: No, no, no, his *name's* Homer Lott. He's *always* in here reading the papers.

*Homer:*   Let's see what sort of a mess the world is in today.

*[He sits down at the newspaper table.]*

*Robin:*   Oh dear, Mr Tremble, some of the books aren't in the right order. Shall I sort them out?

*Oliver:*   If you must. Well, Homer, tell us the worst.

*Homer:*   'Five Hundred Job Losses in Car Factory.' 'More Tax Rises On the Way.'

*Oliver:*   What about the *Boring News*?

*Homer:*   'Sniffer Dog Bites Policeman.'

*Robin:*   That's not boring.

*Oliver:*   No, no, the *Boring News* is the local paper. This is Boring-by-Sea, don't forget.

*Robin:*   Of course, silly me.

*Oliver:*   What else?

*Homer:*   'Planners Run out of Money.' 'Mayor Gets Drunk Again.' Just the usual stuff. Hold on, what's this? 'Purple Wool Mystery.'

*Robin:*   Tell us about that.

*Homer:* All right. *[He reads.]* 'Fifty balls of purple wool were stolen from Hammond's department store yesterday. Store detective I.C.U. Steel says, "I spotted a woman putting the balls of wool into a large shopping bag. She had red hair and dark glasses. When the woman left the shop I asked her to open her bag. To my surprise the bag was empty." The woman gave her name as Olive Branch and her address as 3 Daisy Drive. Police later found that this address did not exist.'

*Robin:* That's terrible. Isn't there any good news?

*Homer:* What about this? 'New Weed Resists All Weed Killers.'

*Robin:* *That's* not good news.

*Homer:* It is for the weed.

*[Enter Charity and Crystal. They have white hair and are wearing purple cardigans. They each have a large shopping bag.]*

*Oliver:* Here come those two old dears who joined the library last week. Good morning, ladies.

*Charity:* Good morning, Mr Tremble.

*Oliver:* This is Robin Banks, our new trainee.

*Charity:*   *So* nice to meet you!

*Crystal:*   We do hope you'll be happy here.

*Robin:*   Thank you.

*Charity:*   Are our cards ready yet, Mr Tremble?

*Oliver:*   Yes. I'll just check that everything is OK. Do you want to watch what I do, Robin?

*Robin:*   Yes, please!

*Oliver:*   Right! I pass this scanner over the card.

*Robin:*   Just like in the supermarket!

*Oliver:*   And the name and address come up on the screen.

*Robin:*   Oh yes, look! Miss Charity Ball, 21 Primrose Park.

*Charity:*   That's me!

*Oliver:*   Are the name and address correct?

*Charity:*   Of *course*. Did you think I'd give you false ones?

*Oliver:*   No, I was just checking. Now, I think I let you take out a book last week.

Charity:  Yes, you did. That was *so* kind of you. Here it is. *100 Knitting Patterns.*

Oliver:  Was it any good?

Charity:  Oh yes! We've each knitted a cardigan.

Crystal:  We're wearing them.

Robin:  I say, you *are* quick workers!

Crystal:  Yes, we are.

Robin:  That purple colour really suits you both!

Crystal:  How nice of you to say so.

Charity:  You can have the book back now.

Oliver:  Thank you.

Charity:  May I choose another one?

Oliver:  You can choose *six* if you like.

Charity:  Oh, I think just one will keep us busy. *[She goes to the shelves.]*

Oliver:  Now, Robin, do you want to check the other lady's card?

Robin:    All by myself? Yes, *please*! Now, I pass the scanner over the card. There we are! Miss Crystal Ball, Twenty-one Primrose Park.

Crystal:    That's me! We're sisters, you see. We've just come to Boring. We moved from the other end of the country, you know.

Oliver:    Primrose Park. Where is that exactly?

Crystal:    Well, it's rather hard to explain. It's sort of . . . tucked away.

Robin:    Did you get a book out last week?

Crystal:    I got out two! Here they are.

Robin:    *Wigs and Disguises* – that looks interesting.

Crystal:    Oh, it was! And so useful too!

Robin:    What was the other book?

Crystal:    This one. *Great Hoaxes of the World*.

Robin:    Was that any good?

Crystal:    Oh yes, it was excellent! Can I keep them both for another week?

Robin:     Yes, that's fine.

Homer:     [*still reading the papers*] There are a lot of deaths
           this week.

Crystal:   Oh dear, are there?

Homer:     Yes. D. Creppit, aged ninety-five. I. B. Old, aged
           one hundred and ten. Foo-Foo the Poodle, aged
           thirteen. Funeral on Wednesday in St Paul's
           Cathedral.

Robin:     A funeral for a poodle?

Homer:     This is no ordinary poodle. It's Lady Hammond's
           poodle. She's mad about animals. You should see
           her Siamese cats. They've all got diamond collars.

Crystal:   Have they? How interesting. We love Siamese cats,
           don't we, Charity?

Charity:   Yes, my dear. They're such a lovely cream colour.
           Do you have a book about them, Mr Tremble?

Oliver:    I'm sure we do. I'll look in the animal section.
           Here, how about this one?

Charity:   *Your Siamese Cat and You* by Isa Blue. That
           sounds good, doesn't it, Crystal? I'll get it out.

*Robin:* Oh good! I'm dying to see how this is done.

*Oliver:* It's easy. Scan the card. Scan the bar code. Then stamp in the date the book is due back.

*Robin:* Can I do that bit?

*Oliver:* Why not? At this rate I'll be able to retire by Christmas.

*Robin:* *[stamping the book]* December twenty-second. There you are, Miss Ball. You've got three weeks.

*Charity:* Oh, we won't need that long. As you said, we're *very* quick workers.

*Robin:* Are you sure you don't want to get out any more books? I see you've both got nice big shopping bags. They're both the same, aren't they?

*Crystal:* Yes, they're *very* handy, aren't they, Charity?

*Charity:* Yes, my dear. Well, goodbye, Mr Tremble.

*Crystal:* Goodbye, Mr Banks!

*Robin:* Goodbye!

*Oliver:* Goodbye, ladies. Don't do anything I wouldn't do!

*Crystal:*  I can't promise that!

   *[Charity and Crystal go out.]*

*Robin:*  What sweet old ladies! I say, Mr Tremble, did I do that all right?

*Oliver:*  Brilliant. You deserve a tea break.

*Robin:*  Oh, I don't think I'd better.

*Homer:*  I wouldn't. It says here: 'Tea Destroys the Brain Cells'.

## SCENE 2: Friday, 8 December

*[Robin is in the library. Oliver comes in.]*

*Oliver:*  Good morning, Robin. You're early again.

*Robin:*  Good morning, Mr Tremble. Do you notice anything different about me?

*Oliver:*  Yes, you've shaved off your moustache. It suits you.

*Robin:*  I didn't have a moustache. No, I mean my badge.

*Oliver:*  Let's have a look. 'I love my library.' Very nice.

Robin:    I'm glad you like it. I've got one for you too. It says, 'Books are cool.'

Oliver:   Er, thanks.

Robin:    Let me pin it on you. *[He pins the badge on to Oliver.]* That looks great!

Oliver:   Where did you get these badges?

Robin:    I made them. I've got a kit.

          *[Enter Homer.]*

Robin:    Good morning, Mr Lott.

Homer:    There's thunder in the air.

Robin:    Would you like a badge? How about this one? 'Your paper, your pal.'

Homer:    No, that's a bit too jolly. Are there any others?

Robin:    Here's a nice one.

Homer:    'Borrow like there's no tomorrow.' That's good advice, you know. I'll have that one.

          *[Robin pins the badge on to Homer. Homer goes to the newspaper table.]*

*Oliver:* Well, Homer, let's have it.

*Homer:* 'Petrol Prices Up Again.' 'Tidal Wave Hits Hungary.'

*Robin:* But Hungary's inland. It hasn't got any sea.

*Homer:* It has now.

*Oliver:* What about the *Boring News*?

*Homer:* 'Chip Shop Closes.' 'Mayor Steals from Washing Line.' The same old stuff. Hold on, this looks a bit more interesting: 'Shee-Shee Stolen.'

*Robin:* Who's Shee-Shee?

*Homer:* One of Lady Hammond's Siamese cats.

*Robin:* The ones with diamond collars?

*Homer:* That's it.

*Robin:* How did that happen?

*Homer:* I'll read it to you. 'On Wednesday Lady Hammond was out at the funeral of her poodle Foo-Foo. A woman rang at the bell. She had blonde curly hair and a wart on her nose. Lady Hammond's maid, Miss Maida Pott, opened the door.'

Oliver:   That reminds me, it's nearly time for tea. Sorry, Homer – go on.

Homer:   'The woman had a bunch of flowers. She asked Miss Pott about Foo-Foo's funeral. When she found she was too late she started to cry. The woman talked to Miss Pott for half an hour. When she left, Miss Pott found that Shee-Shee the cat was missing. A thief had got into the house by the back door and stolen her. Police think that the thief and the woman were working together.'

Robin:   That's terrible.

Oliver:   But not all that surprising.

Robin:   What do you mean?

Oliver:   Never mind.

         [Enter Charity and Crystal.]

Oliver:   Good morning, ladies. Have you finished *Great Hoaxes of the World*?

Crystal:  Yes, thank you. It was excellent! Specially page thirty.

Charity:  Page seventeen was very good too.

*Robin:* Would you like a badge?

*Charity:* How kind of you.

*Robin:* How about this one?

*Charity:* What does it say? I haven't got my reading glasses on.

*Robin:* 'Why beg when you can borrow?'

*Charity:* Oh, very good! Yes, please.

*Crystal:* Do you have another one the same for me?

*Robin:* No, but these two are *nearly* the same. This one says, 'Why *buy* when you can borrow?' and this one says, 'Why *steal* when you can borrow?'

*Crystal:* I'll have 'Why borrow when you can steal?'

*Robin:* No, no, no! You've got it the wrong way round.

*Charity:* Really, Crystal!

*Crystal:* So silly of me – I'm sorry, Mr Banks.

*Robin:* That's all right. Shall I pin the badges on for you?

*Charity:* Yes, please.

Robin:     Oh dear, Miss Ball. You've got some hairs on your nice purple cardigan.

Charity:   How strange. I wonder how they got there.

Oliver:    Are they cream coloured?

Robin:     Yes. How did you guess?

Oliver:    I'll tell you later. I must make that pot of tea first.

           [He goes into the kitchen. He takes Great Hoaxes of the World with him.]

Charity:   We've finished Your Siamese Cat and You too.

Robin:     Was it good?

Charity:   Oh yes, most interesting.

Robin:     What about Wigs and Disguises?

Crystal:   I think we'll need that a little longer.

Charity:   Shall we choose some more books?

Crystal:   Yes, my dear.

           [They go to the shelves.]

Homer:   'Bulgaria Beats England 12–0.' 'Banana Split.'

Robin:   I'm not interested in recipes, Mr Lott.

Homer:   This isn't a recipe. Banana is a rock group and they've just split up.

Charity:   Excuse me, Mr Banks. May I take out a DVD?

Robin:   Yes, but it's eighty pence for a week.

Charity:   I think that's quite good value, don't you, Crystal?

Crystal:   What DVD have you chosen, my dear?

Charity:   *You and Your Van.*

Crystal:   Oh, excellent. Yes, that will be eighty pence *very* well spent. And I've found such an interesting book!

Charity:   What's it called, my dear?

Crystal:   *Great Forgeries of the World.* Here's my card.

Charity:   And here's mine.

Robin:   Thank you. I'm getting quite good at this. *[He scans the cards, books and DVDs. He date-stamps the books.]* The book is due back on December the 29th.

Charity:   Oh, I think you'll be seeing us before then.

Crystal:   Goodbye, Mr Banks. And thank you for the nice badges.

Robin:   Goodbye.

*[Oliver comes back in with a cup of tea.]*

Oliver:   Have they gone?

Robin:   Yes.

Oliver:   Good. I can show you page thirty of *Great Hoaxes of the World*. Listen to this: 'In 1934 a very rich man died in Paris. On the day of his funeral a man came to the house with some flowers. The butler told him that he was too late for the funeral. The man seemed very sad. He stayed on the doorstep a long time, talking to the butler. After he had gone the butler found that another man had broken in and burgled the house.'

Robin:   That's very sad. But why are you telling me about it?

Oliver:   Doesn't it remind you of anything?

Robin:    Of what?

Oliver:   Of Lady Hammond's Siamese cat.

Robin:    Shee-Shee?

Oliver:   Yes. That's just the way *she* was stolen.

Robin:    So you mean someone copied the crime from this book?

Oliver:   Not just *someone* – Crystal and Charity.

Robin:    Mr Tremble! Really! What a thing to say!

Oliver:   Well, what book did they get out last time?

Robin:    *Your Siamese Cat and You.* But that doesn't prove anything!

Oliver:   No? And what about the cream hairs on their cardigans?

Robin:    Well, they said they liked Siamese cats. Maybe they've got one. It doesn't have to be Shee-Shee.

Oliver:   All right, then, what about the purple cardigans?

Robin:    What about them?

*Oliver:* Don't you remember the purple wool that was stolen from Hammond's department store?

*Robin:* Stop this, Mr Tremble, *please*! I won't have it!

*Oliver:* Just listen to page seventeen of *Great Hoaxes*.

*Robin:* Do I have to?

*Oliver:* It won't take long. Here we are, page seventeen: 'In 1922 a store detective saw a woman steal some rings. She hid them in one of her gloves. When the woman left the shop the detective arrested her. But when he looked inside the glove it was empty.'

*Robin:* I don't understand.

*Oliver:* This is what happened: after the woman had stolen all the rings she put her glove down on a counter. Then another woman swapped it for hers. They were partners in crime, you see. Just like Charity and Crystal.

*Robin:* But you couldn't fit fifty balls of wool into a glove.

*Oliver:* No, but Charity and Crystal have got nice big shopping bags. You could fit a lot of wool into *them*.

*Robin:* I'm sorry, Mr Tremble. I just don't believe that

those two nice old ladies would do a thing like that.

Oliver: Think how keen they are on *Wigs and Disguises*. What did they get out this time?

Robin: A DVD about driving vans.

Oliver: Anything else?

Robin: Yes. A book called *Great Forgeries of the World*.

Oliver: Aha! Something's brewing. That reminds me, there's some more tea in the pot. Would you like some?

Robin: No thank you, Mr Tremble. And I do think you should cut down on all this tea. Maybe Mr Lott's right about it destroying the brain cells. It certainly seems to be giving you some funny ideas.

## SCENE 3: Friday, 15 December

*[Robin is in the library. He has some posters. Oliver comes in.]*

Oliver: Good morning, Robin.

Robin: Good morning, Mr Tremble. Could I put up one or two posters?

*Oliver:* Posters? What posters?

*Robin:* Here's one of them.

*Oliver:* Let's have a look. 'Be a bookworm.' Oh yes, very good.

*Robin:* Then there's this one.

*Oliver:* Why has it got a rabbit on it?

*Robin:* Read what it says.

*Oliver:* 'Burrow a book from your library.' I see. Very funny. Where did you get these?

*Robin:* I made them.

*Oliver:* Go on, then, stick them up.

[*Robin starts to stick up the posters. Enter Homer.*]

*Oliver:* Good morning, Homer.

*Homer:* There's black ice on the roads. [*He goes to the newspaper table.*]

*Oliver:* Come on, Homer. Give us the bad news.

Homer:  'Fingernail Found in Fish Finger.' 'Banana Back Together.'

Robin:  That's *good* news, isn't it?

Homer:  Not if you've ever heard their music.

Oliver:  And the *Boring News*?

Homer:  'School Kids Miss Panto Treat.' 'Mayor's Dark Secret.'

Oliver:  Tell us about that.

Homer:  I can't. It's a secret. What's this? 'Forger Steals Van.'

Robin:  Oh no!

Homer:  Oh yes. *[He reads aloud.]* 'On Wednesday, Top Gear Van Hire hired out a white van to a woman. She gave her name as Miss Hazel Twig of 94 Wallflower Way. The woman paid in cash and left her driving licence with Top Gear. When she failed to return the van, Top Gear called the police. They found that the bank notes and driving licence were forged. Also, the address was false. They are looking for a woman with an Afro hairstyle and a limp.'

Robin:      This is terrible! Mr Tremble, you were right all along! Crystal and Charity are a couple of crooks.

Oliver:     You look a bit white, Robin. How about a cup of tea? A nice hot sweet one. They say it's good for shock.

Robin:      Really, Mr Tremble! Tea! Is that all you can think about? We must *do* something!

Oliver:     Like what?

Robin:      Like phoning the police. I don't know why *you* didn't do that before.

Oliver:     You know me, I'm lazy. Anyway, it wasn't as if Crystal and Charity were the great train robbers. They'd only stolen some balls of wool and a cat.

Robin:      You never know *what* they'll stop at. I'm going to phone the police now.

Oliver:     Go on then.

Robin:      All right. *[He dials.]* Police, please. Hello, it's Robin Banks from the library. It's about Charity Ball. No, not the *police* charity ball – no, I *don't* want tickets for that. She's someone you should look into. You should look into Crystal Ball too. No, I'm not a fortune teller. I wish you'd *listen*!

They're two old ladies, and they stole Shee-Shee. They stole the purple wool too, and the van. No, this *isn't* a hoax call. *They're* the hoaxers. Their address? It's 21 Primrose Park . . . You say there's no such address? Well, that proves it! What's that? What do they look like? Well, they've got white hair . . . yes, yes, I know, but she must have been wearing a wig! They've been reading a lot of library books, you see. No, it's *not* me that's been reading too many library books. All right then, be like that. Goodbye. *[He puts down the phone.]* What is the world coming to?

*Homer:*    It's coming to a sticky end if you ask me.

*Oliver:*    Never mind, Robin, you've done your best. Cheer up – it's your last day today. I've bought some jam tarts and Christmas crackers. We can have a little party just before closing time.

*Robin:*    *[still gloomy]* That's very kind of you, Mr Tremble.

*Oliver:*    I'll write a good report about you for head office. And then after Christmas you'll be at a different library. You'll never have to see the Satanic Sisters again.

*Robin:*    *[cheering up a bit]* I hope not.

*[Enter Charity.]*

*Oliver:*    Well, talk of the devil!

*Robin:*    Oh dear! I can't face this. Mr Tremble, do you mind if I go and sort out some books?

*Oliver:*    You do that.

*Charity:*    Good morning, Mr Tremble.

*Oliver:*    Good morning, Miss Ball. And where's your sister today?

*Charity:*    Oh, she was feeling rather tired. It's been *such* a busy week. We've been doing a lot of painting.

*Oliver:*    Have you now? And some driving too?

*Charity:*    How *did* you guess? Oh, of course, the DVD. *You and Your Van. Most* helpful. I've brought it back now. And the book too.

*Oliver:*    Oh yes, *Great Forgeries of the World.* Was that any good?

*Charity:*    Yes indeed, most, er . . .

*Oliver:*    Inspiring?

*Charity:*    You could say that. Especially page sixty-five.

*Oliver:* Have you brought back *Wigs and Disguises*?

*Charity:* My sister still has that. But don't worry, she'll send it back to you.

*Oliver:* Send it? Can't she bring it in?

*Charity:* Not really, Mr Tremble. I'm afraid I have some rather sad news for you.

*Oliver:* Have you?

*Charity:* Well, it's not sad in a *way*. You see, we're going abroad.

*Oliver:* For Christmas?

*Charity:* Oh no, for longer than that. We have to leave in rather a hurry. We're catching the five o'clock car ferry.

*Oliver:* What, today?

Charity. That's right. My sister is busy packing.

*Oliver:* So we won't be seeing you again?

*Charity:* I'm afraid not. We *will* miss Boring-by-Sea. It's such a sleepy little place. And Primrose Park is *such* a nice quiet road.

Oliver:     So quiet no one's ever been there.

Charity:    What was that, Mr Tremble?

Oliver:     Oh, nothing, Miss Ball. Well, I'm sorry you won't be borrowing any more books.

Charity:    It's a shame, isn't it? But do you mind if I have a little read here? You have such a good crime section.

Oliver:     That's fine.

            *[Charity goes over to the crime shelves. Robin is sorting out books.]*

Charity:    Oh, it's you, Mr Banks! You look a bit white. Are you all right?

Robin:      Yes, thank you. *[He drops a pile of books.]*

Charity:    Let me help you pick them up. Oh, this one looks *most* interesting. It's just what I've been looking for. May I have a little look?

Robin:      Er, yes, of course. *[He goes to the counter and whispers with Oliver.]*

Oliver:     Well, what's she reading?

*Robin:*    *Great Kidnappings of the World.*

*Oliver:*   Oh dear, oh dear.

*Robin:*    You don't think . . .

*Oliver:*   Yes, I do. It all fits. They're getting the ferry at five o'clock. She's not taking that book out. She's finding out all she needs to know now. And then she'll go out and . . .

*Robin:*    And *kidnap* someone?

*Oliver:*   Unless someone stops her.

*Robin:*    But we've *tried* telling the police.

*Oliver:*   One of us will have to go out after her.

*Robin:*    Which one?

*[The phone rings. Oliver answers it.]*

*Oliver:*   Hello, Boring Library. Mr Banks? Yes, he's here. It's for you.

*Robin:*    For me? Hello, Robin Banks here. Do we have *what* book? *I Love You?* Who is it by?

*[Charity comes to the counter.]*

Charity: Thank you so much, Mr Tremble. I'll leave the book here, shall I? Well, goodbye, it's been *so* nice knowing you.

Oliver: Goodbye, Miss Ball.

[Exit Charity.]

Robin: [on the phone] Can you hold on a minute, please?

Oliver: It's all right, I'll follow her.

Robin: [to Oliver] Do you really trust me to look after the library? I say, that's wonderful, Mr Tremble.

Oliver: I hope I'll be back in time for our little tea party.

Robin: Goodbye then, and good luck!

[Exit Oliver]

Robin: [on the phone] I'm sorry to keep you waiting. I was just saying good spy – I mean good*bye* to someone. Now, who did you say wrote *I Love You*? William Harry *who*? William Harry Mee? No, I'm not asking you to marry me. I thought you said . . . Hello? Hello? They've hung up.

Homer: They say there's an earthquake brewing.

## SCENE 4: Late Afternoon the Same Day

*[Robin and Homer are in the library. Enter Oliver. He looks worn out.]*

Robin:     Mr Tremble! I'm *so* pleased to see you! I was getting worried. How did you get on?

Oliver:    Put the kettle on and I'll tell you.

Robin:     The tea's all ready. I've put the jam tarts on a plate. Shall I bring it all in here?

Oliver:    Good idea.

           *[Robin goes into the kitchen.]*

Homer:     Have you seen this? 'Dead Man Appears at His Own Funeral.'

Oliver:    Homer, I feel like I'm at *my* own funeral. I'm worn out.

Homer:     Well, I'll be off then.

Oliver:    Have a good weekend. Are you going to see the Christmas lights?

Homer:     How can I? They've all fused.

*[Exit Homer. Robin comes back with the tea, jam tarts and crackers.]*

Robin: Now, Mr Tremble, tell me everything. *Please* tell me they haven't kidnapped anyone.

Oliver: I don't *think* they have. But what a lot of babies there are in this town! I'm beginning to wonder if one less would make much difference.

Robin: Where have you been?

Oliver: Everywhere! I've been following Charity about. She's been all over the place.

Robin: Doing what?

Oliver: Gazing into prams and pushchairs.

Robin: Oh no!

Oliver: Oh yes! And saying 'coochy coochy coo' to all the babies. I was sure she was going to snatch one of them, but she didn't. Then at three o'clock she went to a primary school.

Robin: What did she do there?

Oliver: She waited outside with all the mums. She went up

to a few kids and started chatting to them. But in the end she went away.

Robin:     Where to?

Oliver:    To a phone box. She was in there for ages.

Robin:     And where were *you*?

Oliver:    Hiding in a doorway.

Robin:     Did she see you?

Oliver:    I'm afraid so. After about twenty minutes she popped out. 'Oh, I'm so sorry, Mr Tremble,' she said. 'Did you want to use the phone? I've just got one more call to make.'

Robin:     Did she say who to?

Oliver:    Yes – to a taxi firm, to take her to the ferry port.

Robin:     What did you do then?

Oliver:    I tried to get a taxi and follow her. But I couldn't get one, so I came back here.

Robin:     Mr Tremble, you're a hero! You've prevented a kidnapping. Have a jam tart.

*Oliver:*  Thanks, I will. Now you tell me how *you've* got on.

*Robin:*  Rather well! It was quiet till about half past three. I put some tinsel up round the posters.

*Oliver:*  Very nice too.

*Robin:*  After that it got quite busy.

*Oliver:*  Busy? Boring Library? You must be joking!

*Robin:*  No, I'm not. The phone kept going, and that nice lady from the Schools Library Service came in.

*Oliver:*  What lady?

*Robin:*  The one with the black ponytail.

*Oliver:*  I don't know who you mean.

*Robin:*  You must do. She says she comes here once a month. She did tell me her name. What was it? Oh yes, Holly Hock.

*Oliver:*  I don't know anyone called that. What did she want?

*Robin:*  She'd come to collect the books for the schools.

*Oliver:*    *What?* What books?

*Robin:*    Oh, lots. But she said it was for lots of schools. That's all right, isn't it?

*Oliver:*    Exactly how many books did this lady take away?

*Robin:*    Er, I'm not quite sure. The phone kept ringing, you see.

*Oliver:*    And who was on the phone?

*Robin:*    Well, a lot of different people.

*Oliver:*    Were they all women?

*Robin:*    How did you guess? The funny thing is, they were all asking me about books we didn't have. One lady wanted *Roof Repairs* by Lee King. Then another one asked for by *Storm at Sea* by Gayle Force. I can't remember all the others. I do think you could ask head office for some more new books, Mr Tremble.

*Oliver:*    And all the time you were on the phone this Holly Hock was taking books off the shelves?

*Robin:*    Yes. But it's all right. She gave me a list of them all.

*Oliver:*    Did you look at it?

*Robin:*   Well, no. You see, the phone kept going after she'd left. And then I was getting the tea things ready.

*Oliver:*   Where is this list?

*Robin:*   It's here.

*Oliver:*   Good heavens! She's walked off with all the crime books! And most of the books on travel. And pets. And home decorating.

*Robin:*   Well, maybe the children are doing projects on those subjects.

*Oliver:*   We're talking about five hundred books. How did she take them away?

*Robin:*   Oh, she had a van.

*Oliver:*   A van, did you say?

*Robin:*   Yes, a very nice one. Quite big. White, with 'Schools Library Service' painted on it.

*Oliver:*   Yes. Over the top of 'Top Gear Van Hire'.

*Robin:*   Oh! Oh no! Oh, Mr Tremble, how terrible! You don't think it was . . .

*Oliver:*   Crystal Ball, in one of her 'wigs and disguises'.

Robin:    I can't *bear* this! Please say it's not true!

Oliver:   Keep your hair on. It's bad enough when Crystal takes hers off and changes it every five minutes.

Robin:    But Mr Tremble, we thought it was a *kidnap* they were planning.

Oliver:   That's just what they wanted us to think.

Robin:    I don't get it.

Oliver:   I think I do. They *knew* we knew what they'd been up to. They *wanted* us to know! They were even telling us the page numbers that had given them their ideas. So when Charity started reading that book about kidnapping she knew what we'd think.

Robin:    You mean she was *planning* for one of us to follow her?

Oliver:   She was planning for *me* to follow her.

Robin:    But how did she know it would be you? It could have been me. If you'd stayed behind, the Schools Library trick wouldn't have worked.

Oliver:   That's where the phone call came in.

Robin:    Which one?

*Oliver:* The one that came just before Charity left the library.

*Robin:* The lady who wanted *I Love You* by William Harry Mee?

*Oliver:* Yes. Don't you remember, she asked to speak to *you*?

*Robin:* So you're saying that was Crystal?

*Oliver:* I am.

*Robin:* And what about all those other phone calls?

*Oliver:* That was Charity in the phone box. She was keeping you busy while her sister loaded up the van.

*Robin:* Oh Mr Tremble, I'm so sorry! I feel terrible! What will head office say to me?

*Oliver:* Not as much as they'll say to *me*. I'm the one who left my post.

*Robin:* Oh dear, oh dear! We could both lose our jobs!

*Oliver:* Well, that wouldn't be so bad. We could set up as partners in crime, like Charity and Crystal.

*Robin:* Mr Tremble, *don't*!

*Oliver:* Never mind, let's pull the crackers.

[*They pull one, gloomily. Oliver gets the gift.*]

*Robin:* What have you got?

*Oliver:* A toy van.

[*They pull the other one.*]

*Oliver:* What about you?

*Robin:* A lucky charm. I think it's a Siamese cat.

*Oliver:* Shall we put the paper hats on?

*Robin:* All right.

[*Still gloomy, they put on the hats. The phone rings.*

*Oliver:* Hello. Boring Library. Oh, hello, Miss Ball. What did you say? '*Joyeux Noel*'? What does that mean? Oh, I see, it's the French for Happy Christmas. So you're in France, are you? What? No, I haven't done any Christmas shopping yet. You're giving people books, you say? What a surprise. What was that? Your sister wants to speak to Mr Banks? Here he is. [*He hands the phone to Robin.*]

*Robin:*    Hello . . . What's that? You're writing a book, are you? What, both of you? I see, you're not using your own name. What name *are* you using then? Oh. Well, fancy that. Goodbye.

*Oliver:*   So they're writing a book. What's it called?

*Robin:*    *Great Book Robberies of the World* by M. T. Shelf.

# Persephone

## A play
## by Julia Donaldson

### Twenty-five parts
(can be expanded to include a whole class)

Suitable for top primary

Running time: About forty-five minutes

# Characters

**In the upper world**
Demeter, the goddess of nature
Persephone, her daughter
Pearl ⎫
Coral ⎭ sea nymphs
Hecate, a very old goddess
Apollo, god of sun, music and poetry
Zeus, the king of the gods
Hera, Zeus's wife
Aphrodite ⎫
Athene ⎭ young beautiful goddesses
Hermes, the messenger of the gods
Alexis, a peasant boy
Alexis's mother
a miller
farmers 1, 2, 3 and 4
(Optional) additional non-speaking farmers and peasants

**In the Underworld**
Pluto, god of the Underworld
Cerberus, Pluto's three-headed dog
Nicodemus, Pluto's page boy
servant 1
servant 2
servant 3 (Andros)
cook

# Persephone

## OPENING CHORUS

*[Demeter enters, followed by Alexis and his mother, the millers and the farmers, who carry fruit and corn. (Music on page 215.)]*

Demeter, Demeter,
She makes the apples sweeter,
And everywhere Demeter goes
The grass grows longer,
The plants grow stronger
And everything grows and grows.

Demeter, Demeter,
She makes the peaches sweeter,
And everywhere Demeter goes
The corn turns yellow,
The pears turn mellow
And everything grows and grows.

*[Persephone enters and takes Demeter's hand.]*

The sun shines on the water,
The rain falls on the land
When Demeter and her daughter
Go walking hand in hand.

Demeter, Demeter,
She makes the cherries sweeter,
And everywhere Demeter goes
The roots keep rooting,
The shoots keep shooting
And everything grows and grows.

The countryside looks jolly
In reds and pinks and greens
So it's goodbye melon-cauli,
We're feeling full of beans.

Demeter, Demeter,
She makes the apples sweeter,
And everywhere Demeter goes
The grass grows longer,
The plants grow stronger
And everything grows and grows.

*[The farmers etc. follow Demeter offstage.]*

## SCENE 1: The Sea Nymphs

*[A seashore by a meadow. Persephone and the two sea nymphs, Coral and Pearl, are playing tag on the beach.]*

Coral:          Caught you, Pearl!

Pearl:          Caught you, Coral!

| | |
|---|---|
| *Persephone:* | *[in the meadow]* You can't catch me! |
| *Coral:* | That's not fair, Persephone. |
| *Pearl:* | You're supposed to stay on the beach! |
| *Persephone:* | Why should I? I'm not a sea nymph. |
| *Coral:* | No, but *we* are. |
| *Pearl:* | We can't *live* away from the sea, remember! |
| *Persephone:* | *[coming back to the beach]* Oh, all right, but let's play something different. Let's collect seaweed. |
| *Demeter:* | *[offstage]* Persephone! Persephone! |
| *Coral:* | Your mother's calling you, Persephone. |
| *Persephone:* | Oh no! Just when I'm enjoying myself. Now I'll have to go and help her make things grow. |
| *Pearl:* | That sounds like fun to me. |
| *Persephone:* | Not when you have to do it every day. |
| Demeter: | *[entering]* Persephone! I wish you wouldn't wander off like that. |

| | |
|---|---|
| *Pearl:* | Good morning, Demeter. The flowers are looking lovely today. You must have been working hard. |
| *Demeter:* | Thank you, Pearl – yes, I have. |
| *Coral:* | Why don't you take the morning off? |
| Demeter: | *[laughing]* No, Coral, I can't do that. I have to ripen all the apples today. Come on, Persephone. |
| *Persephone:* | Oh, Mother, do I *have* to come? |
| *Coral:* | Can't she stay here with us, Demeter? |
| *Persephone:* | *Please*, Mother. |
| *Demeter:* | I don't know, Persephone . . . if I let you, you must promise not to— |
| *Persephone:* | I know, I know, not to talk to any strangers. |
| *Demeter:* | And not to eat any food that anyone offers you. |
| *Persephone:* | Oh, Mother, you do go on! |
| *Pearl:* | We'll look after her, Demeter. |

Demeter:        I must say, I'd rather go on my own. Persephone usually eats half the fruit that we ripen.

Persephone:     I can't help it, I *love* fruit. You'll bring me some apples back, won't you?

Demeter:        Yes, Persephone, I will. Now, be good and don't wander off.

Persephone:     No. Goodbye, Mother.

                *[Exit Demeter.]*

Pearl:          Look, here's some of that pretty kind of seaweed. You can have a necklace, Persephone! *[She drapes some seaweed round Persephone's neck.]* There, you look like one of us now!

Coral:          I wish I could have a necklace of flowers, like your mother.

Persephone:     You can! I know where there are lots of flowers!

Pearl:          But, Persephone, you're supposed to stay with us.

Persephone:     I won't go far!

| | |
|---|---|
| *Coral:* | She'll be fine! You sound just like Demeter, the way you go on. |
| *Persephone:* | *[wandering off]* See you soon! |
| *Pearl:* | I hope she'll be all right. |
| *Coral:* | Of course she will! Let's go for a swim till she comes back. |

*[They run off.]*

## SCENE 2: The Capture

*[A meadow. Enter Persephone, picking the petals off a daisy.]*

| | |
|---|---|
| *Persephone:* | Tinker, tailor, soldier, sailor, rich man, poor man, beggar man, thief – oh no, I'm going to marry a thief! |

*[Enter Pluto with Servants 1 and 2.]*

| | |
|---|---|
| *Pluto:* | Good morning, Persephone. *[Persephone looks startled but says nothing.]* Well, don't you have a tongue in your head? Ah, I know, you've been told not to talk to strangers, is that it? But I'm not a stranger. I'm a great friend of your mother, the goddess Demeter, and I'm a god too. My servants will tell you which one. |

Servant 1:     He's Pluto.

Servant 2:     The god of the Underworld.

               *[Persephone backs away.]*

Pluto:         Don't look so shocked, my dear. The Underworld is a very beautiful place.

Persephone:    No it's not, it's a horrible, dark place. I've heard all about it.

Pluto:         Now, now, you mustn't believe all the stories you hear.

Persephone:    But there are no flowers there, and no grass!

Pluto:         Maybe not, but we have jewels that are brighter than any flowers. Come and see, and I'll give you some to keep! Wouldn't you like a diamond necklace instead of this seaweed one?

Persephone:    No!

Pluto:         You'd love my pet as well.

Persephone:    Pet? What pet?

Pluto:         Cerberus, my three-headed dog. I can't wait

to see his tail wagging when he sees the beautiful princess his master has brought back.

Persephone:   You're not *going* to bring me back!

Pluto:   *[holding out his hand]* Persephone! I *beg* you to come with me.

Persephone:   No! Go away!

Pluto:   Now, now, Persephone, I don't want to have to force you. Take my hand.

Persephone:   Help! *[She tries to run but the servants block her way.]*

Pluto:   Seize her!

   *[The servants do so.]*

Persephone:   Let go! Help! Pearl! Coral!

Servant 1:   It's no use struggling.

Servant 2:   You're coming with us.

Pluto:   Hold her tight, but don't hurt her – remember she's going to be your queen.

Persephone:   I'm *not*! Let me go!

| | |
|---|---|
| *Pluto:* | Take her to my carriage. |

*[The servants go out with Persephone, who is screaming and struggling. She takes off her seaweed necklace and throws it to the ground. Pluto follows them out.]*

## SCENE 3: Missing

*[The seashore. Enter Coral and Pearl, who carries a shell bracelet.]*

| | |
|---|---|
| *Pearl:* | Persephone! Look what we've got! A bracelet of shells. |
| *Coral:* | *[snatching the bracelet]* Let *me* give it to her! |
| *Pearl:* | That's not fair! I made it. *[She runs after Coral.]* |

*[Enter Demeter with a basket of apples.]*

| | |
|---|---|
| *Coral:* | Oh, hello, Demeter. Mmm, what lovely-looking apples. Can I have one? |
| *Demeter:* | Yes, of course, help yourselves. But where's Persephone? |
| *Coral:* | Oh, she's around somewhere. |

| | |
|---|---|
| *Demeter:* | What do you mean, 'around'? I can't see her. |
| *Pearl:* | She's picking some flowers for us. |
| *Demeter:* | What? You let her wander off? |
| *Coral:* | We didn't want her to – it was her idea. |
| *Pearl:* | You see, we made a seaweed necklace for her, and she wanted to make some flower ones for us. |
| *Demeter:* | But I *told* you to stay with her. You promised! |
| *Pearl:* | We tried to stop her. |
| *Coral:* | We *couldn't* follow her. We die if we leave the seashore. |
| *Demeter:* | Persephone! Persephone! Where has she got to? |
| *Pearl:* | We'll search the beach, Demeter. |
| *Demeter:* | And I'll look in the meadows. Persephone! Persephone! |

*[They all wander off, calling her.]*

## SCENE 4: The First Clue

*[Evening of the same day. A meadow. Enter Alexis and his mother, who carries a basket of apples.]*

Alexis:      These are the best apples I've ever tasted.

Mother:      Don't eat any more or you'll make yourself sick.

Alexis:      All right, I won't eat them, I'll juggle with them.

Mother:      Stop that – look, you've dropped them, they'll be all bruised now.

Alexis:      *[picking up his apples and spotting Persephone's seaweed necklace]* Look, what's this?

Mother:      It's seaweed – that's strange!

           *[Enter Demeter.]*

Mother:      My goodness, here comes the goddess Demeter. *[She curtsies.]* Greetings, Mother Nature. Alex, stop juggling and get down on your knees.

Demeter:       No, no, let the boy play.

Mother:        Why do you look so sad, madam?

Demeter:       Because I have lost my daughter,
               Persephone. Have you seen her?

Mother:        No, madam, I'm sorry.

Alexis:        I think I might have *heard* her.

Mother:        Don't be silly, Alex – he's always making up
               stories.

Alexis:        It's *not* a story.

Demeter:       Let the child speak.

Alexis:        Well, when I was climbing an apple tree I
               thought I heard someone calling for help . . .
               and there was another sound too.

Demeter:       What was that?

Alexis:        A sort of rattling, rumbling noise – like a
               carriage.

Mother:        Probably just thunder.

Demeter:       What's that you're carrying, child?

| | |
|---|---|
| *Alexis:* | It's some seaweed I found. |
| *Demeter:* | Persephone's seaweed necklace! So she *has* been here. Persephone! Persephone! |
| | *[Demeter goes off.]* |
| *Mother:* | Poor woman! |
| *Alexis:* | I thought you said she was a goddess. |
| *Mother:* | She is, but she's a mother too, just like me. Look at the grass she's been walking on – it's all brown and withered. |
| *Alexis:* | *[biting an apple]* This apple tastes sour! |
| *Mother:* | It must be because Demeter is unhappy. |
| | *[They go off.]* |

## SCENE 5: Hecate

*[A hillside, with the entrance to a cave. It is growing dark. Enter Demeter with a torch.]*

| | |
|---|---|
| *Demeter:* | Persephone! Where are you? Perhaps she's hiding in this cave. Persephone! |

| | |
|---|---|
| *Hecate:* | *[coming out of the cave]* Do I look like Persephone? She's a young girl and I, Hecate, am an old crone. Oh woe! Oh misery! |
| *Demeter:* | What's the matter? |
| *Hecate:* | Don't ask me that! Can't I make moan without everyone asking me what the matter is? Oh woe! Oh despair! Oh tearing out of hair! |
| *Demeter:* | Can't you control yourself a bit? I'm not tearing out my hair and I really do have something to feel miserable about. |
| *Hecate:* | Oh good! Then we can make moan together. Alas, alackaday! |
| *Demeter:* | It's not day, it's night. |
| *Hecate:* | So it is. All right then, alas, alackanight! Well, aren't you going to join in? |
| *Demeter:* | No, I'm too busy looking for my daughter. Persephone! |
| *Hecate:* | You'll never find her. She's probably been eaten by a dragon. Why don't you come into my cave and we can wail together till you are a withered old hag like me! |

| | |
|---|---|
| *Demeter:* | No – I've vowed to take no rest, day or night. I've lit this torch from the fire of the volcano, and it will never go out till Persephone returns. |
| *Hecate:* | In that case, let me go with you, and we can make moan together on the way. |
| *Demeter:* | If you insist. Persephone! Persephone! |
| *Hecate:* | Oh woe! Oh blackest of black beetles! |
| | *[They go off together.]* |

## SCENE 6: The Underworld

*[The Underworld. There is a table and a throne. Andros is setting the table with a plate, knife, fork, spoon, glass and jug. The cook hovers around fussily.]*

| | |
|---|---|
| *Cook:* | Is that table set, Andros? |
| *Andros:* | Nearly. |
| *Cook:* | Hurry up with the food, Nicodemus! |
| | *[Enter Nicodemus with a trolley. On it are three plates of food. A loud barking is heard offstage.]* |

Nicodemus:    That's Cerberus barking! Pluto must be back.

[Enter Pluto, Persephone, Servants 1 and 2 and Cerberus. Everyone else bows. Cerberus leaps around barking.]

Pluto:    Down, Cerberus! Sit! Well, Persephone, what do you think so far? Do you like my Underworld palace?

Persephone:    Not much.

Pluto:    What? Didn't you notice all the golden statues? And look, this is your throne – it's covered in emeralds!

Persephone:    I don't *want* a throne – I'd rather sit on the grass. I want to go home!

Pluto:    Perhaps you don't care for emeralds. But just wait till you see our diamonds. Tell her about them, everyone!

[Pluto and the other underworld characters sing, to the tune of 'Charlie Is My Darling', 'The Underworld Song'. (Music on page 218.)]

Our diamonds are enormous,

Enormous, enormous,
Our diamonds are enormous,
Oh yes, they are.
They're big and bright and beautiful,
They're quite spec-tac-u-lar.
You really ought to see them.

*Persephone:*    I'd rather see a star.

*Pluto and co.:*    Our diamonds are enormous
But she'd rather see a star.

*Pluto [spoken]:*    Perhaps she likes sapphires better than diamonds.

*Pluto and co.:*    Our sapphires are stupendous,
Stupendous, stupendous,
Our sapphires are stupendous,
Oh me, oh my!
They must be even bluer than
The twinkle in your eye.
You really ought to see them.

*Persephone:*    I'd rather see the sky.

*Pluto and co.:*    Our sapphires are stupendous
But she'd rather see the sky.

*Pluto [spoken]:*    See if you can cheer her up, Cerberus.

*[Cerberus jumps up and tries to lick Persephone, who pushes him away.]*

Pluto and co.: Our Cerberus has three heads,
Yes, three heads, yes three heads.
Our Cerberus has three heads,
Upon my word!
And each of them barks louder far
Than any dog you've heard.
You really ought to hear him.

Cerberus: *[vaguely to the same tune]*
Woof woof woof woof woof woof woof
woof!

Persephone: I'd rather hear a bird.

Pluto and co.: Our Cerberus has three heads
But she'd rather hear a bird.

Cerberus: *[angry and disappointed]*
Woof woof woof woof!

Persephone: Take me home, Pluto. I hate it here.

Pluto: Come now, Persephone, I'm sure you'll see
things differently when you've got a good
meal inside you. Cook!

Cook: Yes, Your Majesty.

| | |
|---|---|
| *Pluto:* | What is the first course? |
| *Cook:* | Curried snakes' eggs, Your Majesty. |
| *Pluto:* | Ah, my favourite. |
| *Persephone:* | I don't want any. |
| *Pluto:* | Take it away! |
| *Cook:* | But, Your Majesty! |
| *Pluto:* | You heard what I said. Her ladyship wants to skip the starter. What have we next? |
| *Cook:* | Cockroaches in coal dust, Your Majesty. |
| *Pluto:* | I really can recommend this! |
| *Persephone:* | No! Please! Take it away. |
| *Pluto:* | How about something nice and sweet and sticky? What is the dessert, cook? |
| *Cook:* | Jellied worms with liquorice sauce, Your Majesty. |
| *Persephone:* | That's disgusting! |
| *Pluto:* | What would you like then, my dear? |

| | |
|---|---|
| *Persephone:* | I just want to go home to my mother. *[She starts to cry.]* |
| *Pluto:* | Ah now, I think I *might* be able to help with that. |
| *Persephone:* | What? You'll take me back, you mean? |
| *Pluto:* | Not exactly . . . Pour your mistress out a glass of Lethe water. |
| *Cook:* | Yes, Your Majesty. |
| *Persephone:* | What's this? |
| *Pluto:* | It's some special water from one of my underground rivers. One sip of it will make you forget your mother and the world above. Then you can be happy here with me. |
| *Persephone:* | No! I'd rather be sad and remember my mother than be happy and forget her! |
| *Pluto:* | Very well, my dear, I won't force you. Come, I'll take you on a guided tour – I expect you'll feel hungrier after that. And if not, there's always tomorrow . . . |
| | *[He leads Persephone out. Servants 1 and 2 follow. The cook, Nicodemus and Andros* |

are left to clear away the rejected food,
hampered by Cerberus who bounds about,
trying to eat it.]

## SCENE 7: Apollo

[The following morning. Enter Apollo. He sings (or recites)
'The Sun, the Sun, the Sun'. (Music on page 222.)]

Apollo:       Who turns the night into day?
              The sun, the sun, the sun!
              Who turns the grass into hay?
              The sun, the sun, the sun!
              Who in heaven do you suppose
              Melts all the dewdrops on the rose,
              Paints all the freckles on your nose?
              The sun, the sun, the sun!
              And you're never going to see
              Anyone hotter than me.
              I'm the sun, the sun, the one and only
              Wonderful, wonderful sun!

              [Enter Demeter and Hecate.]

Demeter:      It's Apollo, the sun god.

Hecate:       Oh horrible brightness! Oh hideous light!

Apollo:       Good morning, ladies. What can I do for

|  | you? Would you like a suntan or a few freckles, or have you just come to admire me? |
|---|---|
| *Demeter:* | No, Apollo, I have come to seek news of my daughter, Persephone. |
| *Hecate:* | I keep *telling* you, she's probably fallen off a cliff. |
| *Demeter:* | Do be quiet, Hecate. Apollo, you see everything that happens by day. Tell me, what has happened to Persephone? |
| *Hecate:* | She's been pecked by vultures. |
| *Apollo:* | No such thing. |
| *Demeter:* | So you *have* seen her! Is she alive? |
| *Apollo:* | Certainly, madam, and doing very well for herself. Congratulations. |
| *Demeter:* | What do you mean? |
| *Apollo:* | Your daughter is seated on a throne beside the ruler of the Underworld. |
| *Demeter:* | Pluto! |
| *Hecate:* | I knew it! |

| | |
|---|---|
| *Apollo:* | An excellent match. Allow me to congratulate you in verse. |
| | Oh what a conquest! Oh what a catch!<br>Oh what a fortunate, fabulous match!<br>Oh what a triumph! Oh what— |
| *Demeter:* | Do stop making up poetry and tell me what *happened* exactly. |
| *Apollo:* | Your daughter was picking flowers in the meadow . . . |
| | Pretty maiden<br>Making posies,<br>Picking poppies,<br>Plucking roses . . . |
| *Demeter:* | GET ON WITH IT! |
| *Apollo:* | Pluto spotted her and . . . er, whisked her off to the Underworld. |
| *Demeter:* | In other words, he's *stolen* her. We'll see what the king of the gods has to say about that! Come, Hecate, let's go and complain to Zeus. |
| *Apollo:* | I wouldn't do that, madam. There's little use |

in seeking Zeus . . . that was a good rhyme! Use/Zeus – I must remember that.

*Demeter:* Stop rambling! *Why* can't I get Zeus to rescue Persephone?

*Apollo:* Because he *wants* her to stay in the Underworld.

*Demeter:* How could he?

*Apollo:* Well, you know Pluto has been looking for an Underworld queen for some time.

*Demeter:* No!

*Apollo:* Oh yes. He's been making a terrible nuisance of himself, pestering all the goddesses. They kept complaining to Zeus about it. So when Zeus heard that Pluto had settled down at last, he was delighted.

*Demeter:* This is terrible!

*Hecate:* Oh wringing of hands! Oh gnashing of teeth! Come, Demeter, let's go back to my cave and tear out our hair together.

*Demeter:* No! If Zeus won't help me, I'll have to rescue Persephone myself.

Apollo:    Demeter, don't talk nonsense. You'll never find the entrance to the Underworld. In any case, it's guarded by Pluto's three-headed dog, Cerberus.

Demeter:   I'd tackle a *thirty*-headed dog to get my daughter back. Come on, Hecate, let's go.

Hecate:    I'm sorry, Demeter, I can't take any more of your hope and determination. I'm going back to my cave. You can join me there as soon as you give up.

Demeter:   That will be never!

           *[Hecate and Demeter go their separate ways during Apollo's speech.]*

Apollo:    Poor woman! What sorrow! What bravery! I think I'll make up a poem about it:

           She roams through the land,
           Her torch in her hand,
           Seeking her daughter
           Through fire and through water,
           Her tears making streaks
           On her lily-white cheeks . . .

Oh dear! I'm making myself cry. What about you, ladies? Ladies? They've gone!

*[He shrugs and saunters away.]*

## SCENE 8: Starvation

*[Two people bring on a sign saying 'Six months later'. Enter Alexis and his mother, looking cold, tired and hungry. The miller enters from the other direction.]*

*Alexis:* I'm cold.

*Mother:* I know you are, Alexis – everyone is.

*Alexis:* And I'm hungry too. Why is there no fruit on the trees?

*Mother:* We must make do without fruit. Look, here comes the miller – maybe he can let us have a little flour to make bread with. Good morning, miller.

*Alexis:* I'm not a miller any more. All the wheat in my barn is used up.

*Alexis:* Why don't you get some more?

*Miller:* I can't. No more will grow.

190

| | |
|---|---|
| *Mother:* | Look at the ground – it's frozen solid. |
| | *[Enter Demeter, followed by a group of farmers.]* |
| *Farmers:* | Help us, Demeter. We're starving. Can you do something? |
| *Mother:* | *[down on her knees]* Yes, Mother Demeter, help us! You're the only one who can! |
| *Demeter:* | What is it you want? |
| *Farmer 1:* | We want the plants to grow again! |
| *Alexis:* | We want fruit on the trees! |
| *Miller:* | I need wheat for people to make into bread. |
| *Farmer 2:* | My chickens want corn. |
| *Farmer 3:* | My cows will die without any grass to eat. |
| *Farmer 4:* | We'll *all* die! |
| *All:* | Help us, Mother Nature! |
| *Demeter:* | I *can't* help you. |
| *Alexis:* | Yes you can! I know you can. Remember all |

those juicy apples you used to fill the trees with!

*Demeter:*     *Used* to, child, but not any more. Not since Pluto stole my daughter away. I've given up my other work while I search for her.

*Miller:*     Isn't that a bit hard on us?

*Demeter:*     I *couldn't* help you even if I tried. I'm so unhappy I've lost my power to make things grow.

*Alexis:*     *I'll* help you get Persephone back! I'll fight Pluto.

*Demeter:*     It's no good. Zeus, the king of the gods, is on his side. He wants Persephone to stay in the Underworld.

*Mother:*     What? And for the grass to dry?

*Miller:*     And the corn to shrivel?

*Farmer 1:*     And the fruit to wither?

*Farmer 2:*     And the animals to starve?

*Farmer 3:*     And people to freeze?

| | |
|---|---|
| *Farmer 4:* | And all of us to die? |
| *Demeter:* | It's no use complaining to *me*. Why don't you pray to Zeus instead? |
| *Miller:* | Yes, we'll do that. Zeus! |
| *All:* | Zeus!<br>Bring back the grass!<br>Bring back the corn!<br>Bring back the flowers!<br>Bring back the fruit!<br>Bring back the spring!<br>Bring back the summer!<br>BRING BACK PERSEPHONE! |
| | *[The chant grows louder and louder. They repeat it as they march off.]* |

## SCENE 9: Hide and Seek

*[In the Underworld. Persephone, laughing, runs onstage and hides behind the curtains. Nicodemus, also laughing, runs on, looking for her. (They are playing hide and seek.)]*

| | |
|---|---|
| *Nicodemus:* | Persephone! I know you're here! |
| *Persephone:* | *[jumping out]* Boo! |

*[They both laugh. Pluto enters, carrying some Lethe water.]*

Nicodemus:   Oh, sorry, Your Majesty, we were just . . .

Pluto:   Playing hide and seek, I know. It's good to hear you laugh, Persephone. I do believe you've come to like the Underworld just a little bit.

Persephone:   The caves and twisty passages are good for hide and seek – but I'd still rather be in the open air.

Pluto:   But just one sip of Lethe water could change that!

Persephone:   No, Pluto, I'll never drink that. I don't want to forget my mother.

Pluto:   Then if you'd only eat something. Just a tiny slice of spicy roast mole, perhaps? Or a nice crunchy rock cake? I do so want you to be happy with me.

Persephone:   I know you do, Pluto, and I *have* grown quite fond of you. But I don't even *like* your kind of food. If I was going to eat anything, it would be something fresh and simple.

| | |
|---|---|
| *Pluto:* | Such as? |
| *Persephone:* | Such as a piece of my mother's fruit. |
| *Pluto:* | Why didn't you say so before? |
| *Persephone:* | I haven't said I'll eat it anyway – I promised my mother I wouldn't eat anything. |
| *Pluto:* | I'm sure she wouldn't mind you eating some of *her* food. What a good idea. Nicodemus! |
| *Nicodemus:* | Yes, Your Majesty. |
| *Pluto:* | Go the upper world and pick me some fruit. |
| *Nicodemus:* | Yes, Your Majesty. *[Exits.]* |
| *Persephone:* | I won't eat it! |
| *Pluto:* | I feel sure we can tempt you, Persephone. Now, how about a game of chess? You know how much you love the jewelled chess pieces. |
| *Persephone:* | Will you set me free if I win? |
| *Pluto:* | *[laughing]* You don't give up, do you? |
| *Persephone:* | No, I don't. |

*[They go off together.]*

## SCENE 10: Mount Olympus

*[Two people come on with a sign saying 'Mount Olympus, Home of the Gods'. There is a table, with five goblets and some grapes on it. Zeus is holding a banquet. Seated at the table are his wife Hera, Apollo, Aphrodite and Athene.]*

Zeus:  Some more nectar for you, Athene?

Athene:  Thank you, Zeus, it's delicious.

Zeus:  How about you, Aphrodite? Would you like a top-up?

Aphrodite:  That would be divine.

Hera:  Don't offer *me* any more, will you – I'm only your wife.

Zeus:  Very well, my dear, I won't. Now then, who else – how about Demeter?

Hera:  You *know* she never comes to our banquets.

Zeus:  That's true – what's she up to these days?

Apollo:  Looking for Persephone.

Zeus:  Oh dear, not *still*? It's been six months. I thought she'd have cheered up by now.

| | |
|---|---|
| *Apollo:* | Alas, poor goddess, all forlorn, Wand'ring through the fields of corn . . . |
| *Hera:* | I hate to interrupt, Apollo, but there aren't any fields of corn any more. |
| *Farmers:* | *[off]* Bring back the grass! Bring back the corn! |
| *Zeus:* | Oh no, not that again! I can't stand it. |
| *Aphrodite:* | Just try and ignore it. |
| *Farmers:* | Bring back the flowers! Bring back the fruit! |
| *Zeus:* | I can feel one of my headaches coming on. |
| *Athene:* | Why don't you shoot a thunderbolt at them? That'll shut them up. |
| *Zeus:* | I tried that the other day, and it didn't. |
| *Farmers:* | Bring back the spring! Bring back the summer! |
| *Apollo:* | Would you like me to go and calm them down with some nice poetry? |

| | |
|---|---|
| *Hera:* | They don't want poetry, they want food. |
| *Farmers:* | BRING BACK PERSEPHONE! |
| *Hera:* | Why don't you bring her back, Zeus? Then we'd have a bit of peace. |
| *Zeus:* | What do you other goddesses think? |
| *Aphrodite:* | No, *don't* let her free – Pluto will just come pestering me. |
| *Athene:* | Or me, more likely. |
| *Aphrodite:* | You must be joking! |
| *Hera:* | I can't see why he should fancy either of you. |
| *Zeus:* | Stop that squabbling, my headache's bad enough as it is. |
| *Farmers:* | *[louder]* |
| | Bring back the grass! |
| | Bring back the corn! |
| | Bring back the flowers! |
| | Bring back the fruit! |
| | Bring back the spring! |
| | Bring back the summer! |
| | BRING BACK PERSEPHONE! |

Zeus:        It's no use, I'm going to have to give in. Where's my messenger? Hermes!

Hermes:     *[racing in]* At your command!

Zeus:        Get those wings flapping. I want you to take a message to Pluto.

Hermes:     I go, I go! *[He races out again.]*

Zeus:        Come back! I haven't told you what the message is yet.

Hermes:     *[racing back]* Sorry.

Zeus:        Tell him you've come to take Persephone back to her mother.

Hermes:     I go, I go! *[He races out again.]*

Zeus:        Come *back*! I haven't finished!

Hermes:     *[racing back]* Sorry!

Zeus:        Where was I up to?

Hermes:     Take Persephone's mother back to her.

Zeus:        *No*, you idiot – take Persephone to her

mother – *unless* she's had anything to eat in the Underworld.

Hermes: I go, I go! *[He races away, then comes back.]* I've come back.

Zeus: So I see. That was rather quick, wasn't it?

Hermes: Well, I haven't *been* yet. Er . . . do I have to?

Zeus: Yes, of course. Why?

Hermes: Well, I have the feeling Pluto's not going to be happy about this. He might be angry with me.

Zeus: And *I* might hurl a thunderbolt at you if you don't hurry up and go.

Hermes: I go, I go! *[He races off.]*

Athene: Oh no, now Pluto'll be after me again!

Aphrodite: *Me*, you mean.

Hera: Shut up, you two.

Voices: Bring back Persephone!
Bring back Persephone!
BRING BACK PERSEPHONE!

| Zeus: | *[who has been getting more and more frazzled]* All right, all right! I'm bringing her back! |
|---|---|
| | *[The chanting continues and the gods leave, blocking their ears.]* |

## SCENE 11: Escape

*[In the Underworld, Pluto and Persephone are playing chess.]*

| Persephone: | Checkmate! |
|---|---|
| Pluto: | You've won again! You're too clever for me. |
| Persephone: | So how about setting me free? |
| | *[Cerberus is heard barking in the distance. Nicodemus enters, out of breath, carrying a dried-up pomegranate.]* |
| Nicodemus: | Your Majesty . . . |
| Pluto: | Ah, you're back, Nicodemus. What have you brought? Rosy apples? Juicy pears? |
| Nicodemus: | Er . . . no, Your Majesty. |
| Pluto: | What then? |

| | |
|---|---|
| *Nicodemus:* | Just . . . this! *[He holds out the pomegranate.]* |
| *Pluto:* | What's that supposed to be? |
| *Nicodemus:* | It's a pomegranate, Your Majesty. |
| *Pluto:* | A pomegranate? Would you call that a pomegranate, Persephone? |
| *Persephone:* | Well, it could have been one once, I suppose. |
| *Pluto:* | You hear that! It could have been one once. And you could have been a sensible young man once, instead of a useless halfwit! |
| *Nicodemus:* | But, Your Majesty, let me explain . . . |
| *Pluto:* | Silence! |
| *Persephone:* | Don't be mean, Pluto. Listen to what he has to say. |
| *Pluto:* | Very well, just for you. But it had better be good. |
| *Nicodemus:* | Well, Your Majesty, this was all I could find. All the trees were bare and the plants had died. I couldn't even find a blade of grass. |

Pluto:          What nonsense is this?

Nicodemus:      It's true, Your Majesty. People are saying that Demeter is too sad to make anything grow.

Persephone:     Oh no! My poor mother. Pluto, you *must* let me go back to her.

                [Cerberus is heard barking wildly.]

Pluto:          What's up with Cerberus? I'd better go and see. [Exits.]

Nicodemus:      I'm sorry, Persephone, I really did try to find some nice fresh fruit.

Persephone:     It's all right, Nicodemus. I wouldn't have eaten it anyway . . . though I do love pomegranates.

Nicodemus:      I'm sorry this one's so dried up.

Persephone:     It might not be so dry inside.

Nicodemus:      I'll cut it open. [He does so.]

Persephone:     Oh, I'd forgotten what fruit looked like. It reminds me so much of my mother!

Nicodemus:      Won't you have just a little taste?

Persephone: Well, maybe just a nibble . . . while Pluto's not here. *[She takes a small bite.]* Mmm, I can almost see the upper world.

*[Enter Pluto and Hermes, with Cerberus gambolling around them.]*

Hermes: That's some dog you've got there, Pluto.

Pluto: Sorry about that, Hermes. Down, Cerberus. Are you all right?

Hermes: Yes, just about . . . Actually I'm more frightened of you than of Cerberus.

Pluto: Why, have you brought me bad news?

Hermes: I'm afraid so.

Pluto: Well, don't just stand there! Tell me what Zeus has to say.

Hermes: He says you must . . . give Persephone back.

Persephone: Yes!

Pluto: No! Never! I don't believe it! You're making this up, Hermes. How *dare* you?

| | |
|---|---|
| *Hermes:* | I *knew* you'd be angry! It's not *my* fault, I'm just the messenger. |
| *Pluto:* | So I'm to give up Persephone, just like that? Is there no way of avoiding it? |
| *Hermes:* | Just a moment, there was something . . . what was it? Oh yes, that's it. You *can* keep Persephone here if she's had anything to eat while she's been with you. |
| *Pluto:* | I see. |
| | *[Persephone looks at Nicodemus and puts her finger to her lips.]* |
| *Hermes:* | Well, has she? |
| *Pluto:* | I can't lie. She's refused everything I've offered her. |
| *Hermes:* | *[turning to Persephone]* Then you're to come with me! |
| *Persephone:* | When can we go? |
| *Hermes:* | Straight away! *[He starts to charge out.]* |
| *Persephone:* | Wait a second, I must say goodbye. *[Pluto has his back turned.]* Goodbye then, Pluto. |

Don't look so sad! Maybe I can come back and visit you . . .

Pluto: Who do you think you're fooling? Demeter will never let you out of her sight again.

Persephone: Well, goodbye anyway. All right then, Hermes, I'm ready.

Nicodemus: Aren't you going to say goodbye to *me*?

Persephone: Nicodemus, of course! How could I forget? I'll always remember our games of hide and seek.

Hermes: Do come on, Persephone. I'm getting itchy feet.

Persephone: All right, let's go!

*[Hermes takes her hand and they race out together.]*

Nicodemus: Shall I clear the table, Your Majesty?

Pluto: Yes. No, wait! Let me taste a morsel of the pomegranate first. It could make Persephone feel nearer.

Nicodemus: Yes, Your Majesty.

| | |
|---|---|
| *Pluto:* | What's this? It's already been cut open. Someone's eaten a bit. Was it you? |
| *Nicodemus:* | No, Your Majesty. |
| Pluto: | Who then? Speak! Was it Persephone? *[Nicodemus is silent.]* It *was*, wasn't it? |
| *Nicodemus:* | She just had a mouthful, Your Majesty. She can't have eaten more than six seeds. |
| *Pluto:* | This changes everything! |
| *Nicodemus:* | Where are you going? |
| *Pluto:* | After them, of course, and you're coming with me. Persephone has eaten in my kingdom. She's mine forever! |

*[He goes out, pulling Nicodemus with him.]*

## SCENE 12: The Judgement

*[The seashore. Demeter is wandering around, looking tired. Her torch has gone out but she has not noticed this. Enter Coral and Pearl.]*

| | |
|---|---|
| *Coral:* | Good morning, Demeter. |
| *Pearl:* | Still no sign of Persephone? |

| | |
|---|---|
| *Demeter:* | No. |
| *Coral:* | Don't you ever rest? |
| *Demeter:* | No. I will search and this torch will burn until Persephone returns. |
| *Coral:* | But your torch *isn't* burning. |
| *Demeter:* | How strange! It's gone out – can Zeus be playing tricks on me? |
| *Pearl:* | Look, here's a daisy. |
| *Demeter:* | That's impossible. |
| *Coral:* | And another one. |
| *Demeter:* | I don't understand this. |
| | *[Persephone runs onstage.]* |
| *Persephone:* | Mother! |
| *Demeter:* | Persephone! Am I dreaming? |
| *Persephone:* | No, it's really me! Zeus sent Hermes to bring me back. |
| *Hermes:* | *[entering, laughing]* It felt more like you |

bringing me! I could hardly keep up, even with the wings on my heels.

Persephone: *[hugging Demeter]* Oh, it's so good to see the grass again! Nicodemus said it had all died.

Hermes: It had, but everywhere you tread it's been springing back again.

Pearl: Persephone! We've missed you so much!

Coral: Was it terrible in the Underworld?

Persephone: It wasn't so bad once I got used to it. Pluto was very kind to me.

Demeter: Kind! How could you call him kind when he stole you away from me?

Persephone: But he was so lonely, Mother. I helped to cheer him up.

Coral: What does he look like? Is he very ugly?

Persephone: No, he's tall and proud-looking, and he always dresses in fine clothes and jewels.

Pluto: *[entering, followed by Nicodemus]* Just like this!

| | |
|---|---|
| *Persephone:* | Pluto! |
| *Demeter:* | What are you doing here! |
| *Pluto:* | I have come for Persephone. |
| *Demeter:* | No! She belongs here! |
| *Hermes:* | Remember Zeus's command, Pluto. |
| *Pluto:* | Yes, I *do* remember Zeus's command. Persephone could return, provided she had eaten nothing. |
| *Hermes:* | Well? You told me yourself she had refused everything you offered her. |
| *Pluto:* | Everything except this! *[He holds out the pomegranate half.]* |
| *Demeter:* | You're making this up, Pluto. I'm sure my daughter wouldn't want such a shrivelled-up pomegranate. Would you, Persephone? |
| *Pluto:* | Well, Persephone? |
| *Persephone:* | Nicodemus, you told him! |
| *Nicodemus:* | I'm sorry, Persephone. I *meant* to keep it a |

secret, but I found I couldn't lie to Pluto, and . . . I wanted you back too.

Demeter: So it's true!

Persephone: It was only a little nibble. I'm sure it doesn't really count!

Pluto: Come with me, Persephone.

Demeter: No, she's staying here.

Zeus: [entering] What are you trying to do – tear the poor girl in half?

Everyone: Zeus!

Zeus: Hermes, have you muddled up my message? It was only Persephone you were supposed to bring back from the Underworld, not Pluto as well.

Pluto: Persephone is mine! She has eaten with me, and now she must stay with me.

Demeter: But all she ate was six seeds of a pomegranate – one of *my* pomegranates!

Zeus: Persephone, is this true?

*Persephone:*     Yes, it is.

*Zeus:*     Very well. For every seed you ate you must spend one month of each year underground with Pluto.

*Demeter:*     No! I can't part with Persephone again!

*Zeus:*     Wait – but for the other six months she shall stay here with you.

*Demeter:*     Am I to lose you for half of every year?

*Persephone:*     Don't be so sad, Mother. I'll be glad to keep Pluto company.

*Pluto:*     I'll look after her, Demeter.

*Nicodemus:*     And she can play hide and seek with me.

*Persephone:*     It won't be so bad next time – you'll know that I'll be coming back.

*Demeter:*     Very well, Zeus. But when Persephone is away, the plants will die and the seeds will stay buried in the earth. We shall call it winter.

*Pearl:*     Don't think of that time yet, Demeter – Persephone's six months on earth are only just beginning.

Persephone:    We've got the whole summer to look forward
               to!

               [*Farmers, miller, Alexis and his mother and
               two Underworld servants enter with flow-
               ers, fruit and corn.*]

All:           Demeter, Demeter,
               She makes the apples sweeter,
               And everywhere Demeter goes
               The grass grows longer,
               The plants grow stronger
               And everything grows and grows.

               [*Enter Hecate, followed by remaining char-
               acters.*]

Hecate:        Can't you turn the jollification down? I can't
               hear myself moan.

Demeter:       Never mind your moaning, Hecate.
               Persephone's back. Come and celebrate with
               us.

Hecate:        Oh all right, just this once, but I'll have to
               moan extra hard afterwards to make up
               for it.

All:           Demeter, Demeter,
               She makes the peaches sweeter,

And everywhere Demeter goes
The corn turns yellow,
The pears turn mellow
And everything grows and grows.

The sun shines on the water,
The rain falls on the land
When Demeter and her daughter
Go walking hand in hand.

Demeter, Demeter,
She makes the cherries sweeter,
And everywhere Demeter goes
The roots keep rooting,
The shoots keep shooting
And everything grows and grows.

The countryside looks jolly
In reds and pinks and greens
So it's goodbye melon-cauli,
We're feeling full of beans.

Demeter, Demeter,
She makes the apples sweeter,
And everywhere Demeter goes
The grass grows longer,
The plants grow stronger
And everything grows and grows.

# Demeter, Demeter

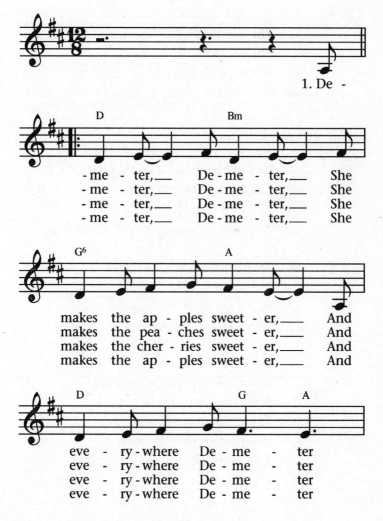

1. De -

-me - ter,___ De - me - ter,___ She
-me - ter,___ De - me - ter,___ She
-me - ter,___ De - me - ter,___ She
-me - ter,___ De - me - ter,___ She

makes the ap - ples sweet - er,___ And
makes the pea - ches sweet - er,___ And
makes the cher - ries sweet - er,___ And
makes the ap - ples sweet - er,___ And

eve - ry - where De - me - ter
eve - ry - where De - me - ter
eve - ry - where De - me - ter
eve - ry - where De - me - ter

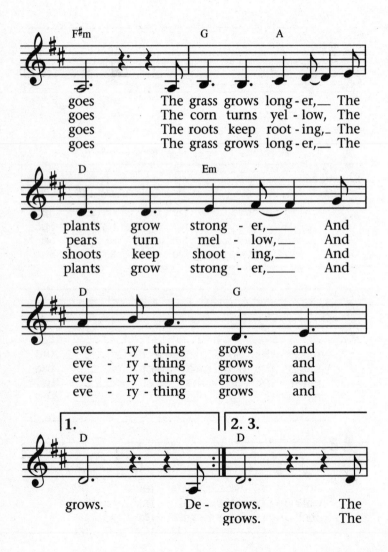

sun shines on the wa - ter,___ the
count - ry - side looks jol - ly___ In

rain falls on the land When De -
reds and pinks and greens, So it's

-me - ter and her daugh - ter___ Go
good - bye me - lon - cau - li,___ We're

walk -ing hand in hand. De - grows.
feel - ing full of beans. De -

# The Underworld Song

Our dia-monds are e - nor - mous, e-
Our sap-phires are stu - pen - dous, stu-

-nor - mous, e - nor - mous. Our
-pen - dous, stu - pen - dous. Our

dia - monds are e - nor - mous, Oh
sap - phires are stu - pen - dous, Oh

yes, they are. They're big and bright and
me, oh my! They must be e - ven

beau - ti - ful, They're quite spec-tac - u-
blu - er than the twin - kle in your

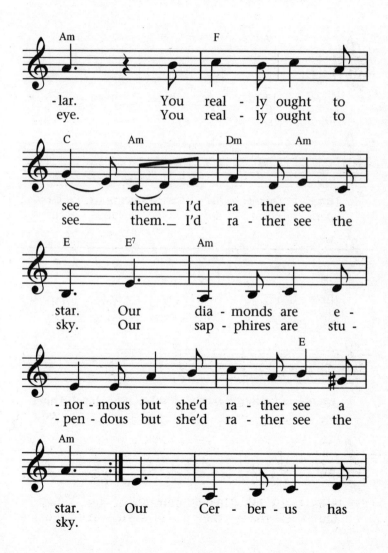

-lar.       You   real - ly ought    to
eye.       You   real - ly ought    to

see_____ them._ I'd  ra - ther see   a
see_____ them._ I'd  ra - ther see   the

star.    Our        dia - monds are   e -
sky.     Our        sap - phires are   stu -

- nor - mous but she'd  ra - ther see   a
- pen - dous but she'd  ra - ther see   the

star.    Our        Cer - ber - us  has
sky.

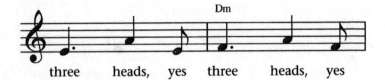

three    heads,   yes    three    heads,   yes

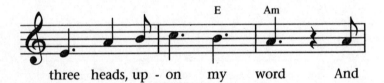

three    heads.   Our   Cer - ber - us    has

three   heads, up - on    my    word    And

each    of them   barks   loud - er   far   than

a  -  ny   dog   you've   heard.        You

real - ly ought to hear___ him. Woof

woof, woof woof, woof woof, woof woof_ I'd

ra - ther hear a bird. Our

Cer - ber - us has three heads but she'd

ra - ther hear a bird.

# The Sun, the Sun, the Sun

Who turns the night in-to day? The

sun! The sun! The sun!

Who turns the grass in-to hay? The

sun! The sun! The sun!

Who in Hea-ven do you sup-pose

melts all the dew drops on the rose?

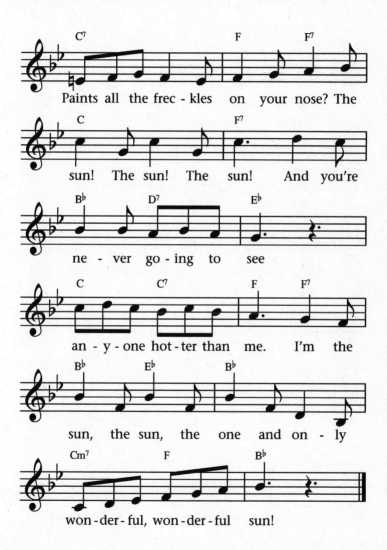

Julia Donaldson

# Princess MIRROR-BELLE

**'I'm Princess Mirror-Belle.
You really ought to curtsy,
but as you're my friend I'll
let you off.'**

Ellen has a big surprise when she looks into her bathroom mirror – and sees a mysterious girl. It can't be her reflection because reflections can't talk back to you! The girl says her name is Mirror-Belle and that she's a princess from a magical, faraway place.

Soon Mirror-Belle and Ellen are friends. But Mirror-Belle is very naughty and is about to lead Ellen into all kinds of amazing and exciting adventures . . .

Six delightfully funny stories from the much-loved and bestselling author of *The Gruffalo*.

# Julia Donaldson
# Princess
# MIRROR-BELLE
## and the Magic Shoes

**'They're magic shoes,'**
**Princess Mirror-Belle said.**
**'As soon as I put them on,**
**my feet start dancing and**
**I can't stop.'**

Ellen will never get used to having mysterious Mirror-Belle as her friend. After all, what other friend appears from a mirror and says she is a princess from a magical and distant land?

Now mischievous Mirror-Belle is back – a surprise visitor at Ellen's ballet class. And she's all set to dance Ellen into all sorts of amazing adventures!

Five new delightfully funny stories starring naughty Princess Mirror-Belle!

*Poems by Julia Donaldson*

*Crazy Mayonnaisy Mum* is packed with all sorts of poems and rhymes, including a sequence of number rhymes, action rhymes, noisy rhymes and more thoughtful pieces too. A real joy.

## Noisy Garden

If tiger lilies and dandelions growled,
And cowslips mooed, and dog roses howled,
And snapdragons roared and catmint miaowed,
My garden would be extremely loud.

# A selected list of titles available from Macmillan Children's Books

The prices shown below are correct at the time of going to press.
However, Macmillan Publishers reserves the right to show new retail
prices on covers, which may differ from those previously advertised.

---

**Julia Donaldson**

| | | |
|---|---|---|
| Princess Mirror-Belle | ISBN-13: 978-0-330-41530-9 | £3.99 |
| | ISBN-10: 0-330-41530-1 | |
| Princess Mirror-Belle and the Magic Shoes | ISBN-13: 978-0-330-43329-7 | £3.99 |
| | ISBN-10: 0-330-43329-6 | |
| Princess Mirror-Belle and the Flying Horse | ISBN-13: 978-0-330-43795-0 | £3.99 |
| | ISBN-10: 0-330-43795-X | |
| Crazy Mayonnaisy Mum | ISBN-13: 978-0-330-41490-6 | £3.99 |
| | ISBN-10: 0-330-41490-9 | |

---

All Pan Macmillan titles can be ordered from our website,
www.panmacmillan.com, or from your local bookshop
and are also available by post from:

**Bookpost, PO Box 29, Douglas, Isle of Man IM99 1BQ**
Credit cards accepted. For details:
Telephone: 01624 677237
Fax: 01624 670923
Email: bookshop@enterprise.net
www.bookpost.co.uk

**Free postage and packing in the United Kingdom**